Doors of Perception

— icons and their
spiritual significance

Doors of Perception

— icons and their spiritual significance

by

JOHN BAGGLEY

with an Appendix by

RICHARD TEMPLE

MOWBRAY
LONDON & OXFORD

Text copyright © John Baggley 1987
Appendix © Richard Temple 1987
Plate reproductions 1–17 copyright Temple Gallery

First published 1987 by A.R. Mowbray & Co Ltd
Saint Thomas House, Becket Street, Oxford OX1 1SJ

Typeset by Dentset, 35 St Clements, Oxford OX4 1AB
Printed in Great Britain by Cowells Ltd. of Ipswich

British Library Cataloguing in Publication Data
Baggley, John
Doors of perception: icons and their
spiritual significance
1. Icons
I. Title
704.9′482 N8187

ISBN 0–264–67118–X
ISBN 0–264–67012–4 Pbk

I saw a door open in heaven

Revelation 4.1

The icon is a door.
Life of St Stephen the Younger (died 765)

Art does not render the visible;
rather it makes visible.

Paul Klee (1879–1940)

CONTENTS

CONTENTS

ACKNOWLEDGEMENTS

Many people have helped in the preparation of this book, and to them I owe a debt of gratitude. Michael Trend and Nicholas Gendle have given much assistance with the text. Richard Temple has not only written the appendix on icon painting and provided most of the illustrations but been a stimulus and inspiration in so many other ways. The preparation of the text would have been impossible without the word-processing skills of Dr Elizabeth Taylor, and the initial work of writing would not have been possible without the hospitality of David and Janet Mellor and Anthony Symondson. Kenneth Baker of Mowbrays has been a patient and encouraging source of support throughout the time this book has been in preparation. Many other friends and colleagues have unwittingly contributed by their interest, curiosity, and questioning, and their recognition of the potential importance of icons for the developing spirituality of the Western Church. Friends in the Serbian Orthodox community in Bicester have also been an encouragement, partly through their amazement that an Anglican priest should have an interest in icons, and partly because the common interest in icons has proved a visual meeting point that has circumvented the linguistic problems of communication between people of very different languages.   J.S.B

The Author and Publisher wish to thank the following for their kind permission to quote material from the works listed:

Faber and Faber Ltd: *The Festal Menaion* and *The Lenten Triadon*, translated by Mother Mary and Archimandrite Kallistos Ware and *The Philokalia*, Volume 1, translated by G.E.H. Palmer, Philip Sherrard and Kallistos Ware.

William Heinemann Ltd: Procopius, *History of the Wars*, Volume VII, translated by B.H. Dewing.

Lutterworth Press: *New Testament Apocrypha*, Henneke, 1963.

Oxford University Press: Kallistos Ware, *Eastern Churches Review*, Volume 8, No. 1.

Paulist Press: John Climacus, *The Ladder of Divine Ascent*, translated by Colin Luibhead and Norman Russell, Classics of Western Spirituality Series, © 1982 by The Missionary Society of St Paul the Apostle in the State of New York; Origen, *An Exhortation to Martyrdom*, translated by John J. O'Meara, Ancient Christian Writers Series, © 1954 by the Revd Johannes Quasten and the Revd C. Plumpe; and *Philo of Alexandria*, translated by David Winston, Classics of Western Spirituality Series, © 1981 by David Winston.

Paulist Press and SPCK: Gregory of Nyssa, *The Life of Moses*, translated by Abraham J. Malherbe and Everett Ferguson, Classics of Western Spirituality Series, © 1978 by the Missionary Society of St Paul the Apostle in the State of New York.

Penguin Books Ltd: Timothy Ware, *The Orthodox Church* (Pelican Books, 1963, revised edition 1964), © Timothy Ware, 1963, 1964; Maxim Gorky, *My Childhood*, translated by Ronald Wilks (Penguin Classics, 1966), © Ronald Wilks, 1966.

Sagittarius Press: *The Painters Manual of Dionysius*, translated by Paul Hetherington 1981.

Saint Vladimir's Seminary Press, Crestwood, New York 10707: N. Cabasilas, *The Life in Christ*, 1974; St Theodore the Studite, *On the Holy Icons*, translated by Catherine P. Roth; and L. Ouspensky, *Theology of the Icon*.

SCM Press Ltd: John Oulton and Henry Chadwick, *Alexandrian Christianity*, SCM Press, 1954.

SPCK: *The Orthodox Liturgy*, 1964.

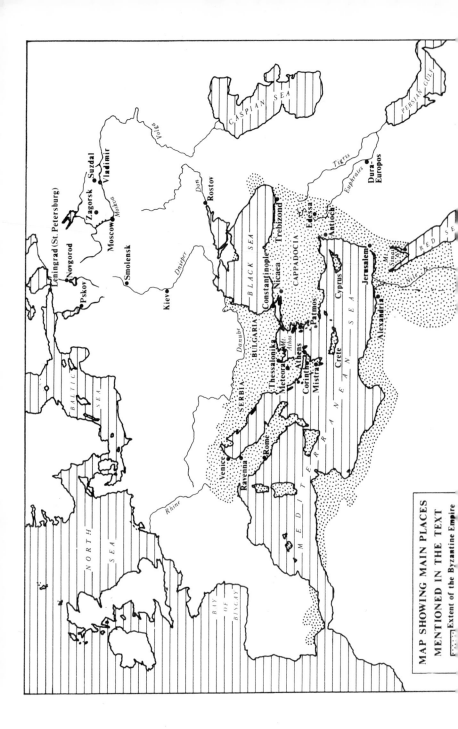

MAP SHOWING MAIN PLACES
MENTIONED IN THE TEXT

.... Extent of the Byzantine Empire

PREFACE

It may well seem strange that an Anglican parish priest should write an introductory book on icons. After all, icons are hardly a part of the English Christian tradition. The tradition to which icons belong is a complex one, and one that is alien to many Western Christians. My own love of icons goes back over twenty years, and probably started with a recognition of the strange stillness and attentiveness that is present in many icons. My interest has deepened through study of the history of icons and their place in the Eastern Orthodox tradition of theology and spirituality. Icons are part of a tradition of spiritual communication that values the visual side of human perception as well as the verbal aspect. It is my experience that many Western Christians are pleasantly surprised to discover the richness of the tradition that lies behind any single icon. The approach I have used in this book involves looking at some aspects of the history of Orthodox Church art, looking at the biblical material and the way it has been used, and exploring the spiritual tradition within which the great flowering of icon-painting took place. I hope this is an approach which others will find helpful, and which will stimulate them to engage in further study and exploration.

It is easy for Western Christians to be either scathingly critical of the Orthodox Churches, or else to be romantically idealistic about them. 'Timelessness' is a word often used in relation to the Orthodox Church, either as a commendation of its sense of the holy and the continuing tradition of the Church, or else as a condemnation of its failure to face up to political and social issues in a rapidly changing world. I believe it is important to honour the great theological and spiritual traditions of Orthodoxy (particularly as manifested in icons and the liturgy), while at the same time being neither callously critical nor naively romantic about the life of parts of Eastern Christendom whose historical background is alien to that of the Western Churches.

When noise and movement are increasingly dominating our world — and often our churches as well — I believe it is important we should cherish those things that bring silence and stillness into our lives. I believe it is this need for a depth of silence and stillness that has led many Western Christians to discover in the icons of the Orthodox Churches a means of entering into the stillness of heart where God can be known and loved. I pray that this book will help others to enter into that stillness, knowledge and love.

J.S.B.

Chapter One

A WAY IN

The word 'icon' is generally used to describe those religious pictures — mainly portable wood panel paintings — which have a prominent place in the life and worship of the Eastern Orthodox Churches. The word comes from the Greek εικων meaning image; it is the word used in the Greek Bible in Genesis chapter one, where we are told that man is made in the image of God; and the same word is used when St Paul speaks of Jesus Christ being the image of the invisible God in the Epistle to the Colossians. The word 'icon' thus leads us to explore both the painting of these holy pictures, and the faith that they enshrine and represent.

To many people with a Western European background of religion and art, icons have seemed to be odd paintings; they have often been dismissed as insignificant with such unflattering descriptions as 'flat', 'dark', and 'primitive'; the lack of 'realism' in icons has also been a major problem for Western people. Only slowly has interest penetrated through to the more ancient traditions and works of Christian icon painting. Layers of mental and spiritual misunderstanding have had to be penetrated, as well as layers of dirt and over-painting on the icons themselves, before the true glory and wonder of the great tradition of icon painting could be revealed. The work of scholars, restorers, and men of prayer has opened up the doors of perception, and now we can enter into the world of the holy icons with a sense of wonder and awe; this entry into the world of the icons can at the same time be an entry into our own interior life, a passing through the 'narrow gate' that leads to Life.

Various external developments in our society have helped Western Christians to become increasingly aware of icons in recent years; television programmes and many books have created a popular interest; travel into Russia, Greece, Cyprus and other eastern Mediterranean countries has enabled many people to see icons in Orthodox Churches as well as in

1

museums; and the presence of ex-patriate Russian and Greek Orthodox communities in England, France and the United States has done much to stimulate interest in Orthodoxy among Western Christians. However, three other and more profound reasons for the current Western interest in the Orthodox tradition should be recognized.

First, it is a Christian tradition with a strong intuitive element; this is in marked contrast to the rational, intellectual, and cerebral elements in much of Western Christianity, where the written or spoken word has become the primary means of religious perception and communication. The growing interest in Orthodoxy is part of a search for a fuller perception of God and the Faith of the Church, a perception that does justice to other parts of the human psyche or personality. The head and the intellect need to be balanced by the heart and its intuition.

Second, there is a recognition that in the Orthodox Churches we see major Christian bodies which have not been dominated by the same historical events as the Western Church. The controversies of the Reformation, Counter-Reformation and the Enlightenment have profoundly influenced Western Christian thought during the last 400 years. Within Orthodoxy, the historical developments have been very different, and in studying the faith and life of these Churches we have to leave behind some of the commonly held assumptions of Western Christianity. This does not mean that Western Christians should simply abandon their own history and rich tradition of spirituality; nor does it mean that the Eastern Churches are free of conditioning by factors in their history; but it does open up a series of different attitudes and assumptions about the faith, prayer and worship of the Church. If the Ecumenical movement has any significance at all, it means we have to enter into the memory, history and experience of Christian traditions that are different from our own; only then can we discover the depths at which we are united and recognize some of the reasons for misunderstanding, disagreement, and division.

Third, there has recently been a great interest in Orthodox spirituality. It is as if something from the Christian East has been offered to the Christian West at a time when the spiritual searches of many Western people have been likely to by-pass Christianity altogether. In monastic circles there has been a considerable meeting of Eastern and Western traditions, and in many European monasteries icons now have a prominent position as focal points of devotion alongside or in place of the statues that have long been important visual aids to devotion in Western Churches. In liturgical matters, much Western reform has been saved from arid intellectualism by the influence of Orthodox traditions mediated into the Western Churches through places like Chevetogne in Belgium, St Vladimir's Seminary in New York, and the ecumenical community at Taizé in France. And at the level of private prayer and devotion, the Jesus Prayer — one of the corner-stones of Orthodox spirituality — has become an increasingly significant element in Western teaching and practice. The Orthodox theological and spiritual traditions also raise the issue of the significance of matter, which is not only a perennial problem for philosophers and spiritual writers, but is a crucial question facing many Western Churches today; the current pressures and temptations to idolize the material world are enormous, and come at a time when many Christians have lost a sacramental vision of the world; a spirituality that does not do justice to the world of matter and creation does not deserve to be called Christian. The search for spirituality can often involve a fundamental split between matter and spirit, the secular and the sacred, and an abdication by Christians of a proper concern for the world of political and social affairs. In spite of failures in this respect by the Orthodox Church its theology and spirituality uphold the doctrines of Creation and the Incarnation, and the use of icons particularly upholds the inter-relatedness of matter and spirit in a world where we easily allow them to be become divorced.

This book is written from within the Western Christian tradition, and primarily with Western Christian readers in mind. It is intended to foster the interest in icons that already exists among many Western Christians, and to take that interest beyond the level of merely looking at religious pictures. 'The icon is a door', we are told; and a door is meant to be passed through, to be the threshold across which we pass into a different place. This book is intended as a way in to what for many is still the unfamiliar world of icons and Eastern Orthodoxy; some landmarks are brought into focus, and some sign posts are established. The territory to be explored requires that some work be done on history, theology, and imagery, but this is external, introductory work. The real territory to be explored is the human heart. Our own, yes; but also the heart of that transfigured humanity that we see in Christ and his saints. Icons form a door into the divine realm, a meeting point of divine grace and human need; moreover, they are also a way by which we enter more deeply into our own interior life. And that journey, that exploration is aided by considering the icons from the different standpoints of history, theology, imagery and spirituality.

The first two chapters explore some of the historical background necessary to understand the Orthodox world in which icon painting has flourished, particularly the origins of Christian iconography, and the major turning points as that iconography developed within the Byzantine Empire. The next two chapters are concerned with imagery in the Bible, the way this 'translates' into the visual language of iconography, the importance of allegorical interpretation of the Scriptures, and the influence of Alexandrian Christianity on the way theology and spirituality developed in the early centuries of the Church's history. The chapter on the spirituality of the icon painters is important for an understanding of the pattern of prayer that is enshrined within the great icons, and leads on to a chapter on the visual language of the icons, in which particular details of the ways in which icons 'speak' to us are investigated. The final chapter sets the icons in the context of Orthodox church buildings, worship, and society. The appendix deals with some technical details about icon painting and its history.

The plates and commentary are intended to be something which readers can make use of in their own prayer and reflection, as well as being referred to at appropriate points of the text. Many of the quotations used may well be unfamiliar

to some readers. Quotations in the chapter on biblical
interpretation may require reading more than once before
their sense becomes obvious. The quotations in the chapter on
the spirituality of the icon painters, particularly those from St
John Climacus and *The Philokalia* deserve to be given as much
patient reflection and meditation as the plates of the icons
themselves; the texts of these spiritual writers were intended
to be pondered at length, and should not be treated merely as
writings that illustrate a particular point in the argument of
this book.

The quotations from the *Painter's Manual* of Dionysius of
Fourna help to illustrate both detailed iconography and also
the strong sense of holy tradition that is integral to the life of
the Orthodox Churches. The *Painter's Manual* comes from the
eighteenth century, when the profound inspiritation behind
the great tradition of icon painting was being eroded by
Western influences, and the art of icon painting was becoming
a rather ossified tradition that perpetuated formal designs.
Even so, the *Painter's Manual* is interesting evidence of the way
an eighteenth century icon painter saw himself in a theological, artistic and spiritual tradition that had its roots far back
in history in the early days of the Christian Church.

The plates in this book are nearly all of icons which have
been exhibited in the Temple Gallery, London. The Revised
Standard Version of the Holy Bible has been used in
quotations throughout this book. The map is intended to
provide an easy means of locating the places mentioned in the
text, and also an indication of the geographical extent of the
Orthodox Church life during the period of the Byzantine and
Russian Empires. The dates of some saints mentioned are
given in the texts; others may be found at the index entry. The
works listed in the bibliography will enable readers to move
on from this book to a more detailed study of the Orthodox
Church's faith, history, spirituality and art that are enshrined
and exemplified in the holy icons.

Chapter Two

HISTORICAL
BACKGROUND
Beginnings and early developments

I

For many Orthodox Christians there is a great sense of permanence about the Church, the liturgy and the Christian faith; what has been revealed has a timeless quality; it is concerned with the things of God and eternity and man's place in the scheme of things. It seems quite natural to Orthodox Christians to believe that icons have always been a part of Church life from the earliest days; icons have always been 'there' in the same way that for Western Christians in a Protestant tradition the Bible has always been 'there'. It is almost inconceivable for each of these different groups of Christians that there could have been a time when the Church was without icons or without the Bible.

The eighteenth century Greek icon painter Dionysius of Fourna in his *Painter's Manual* speaks of the holy and venerable nature of the task in which icon painters are engaged:

'Work well, my friend, without sparing your efforts, but with the utmost diligence and care, so that you may be taught this art and master it completely; for this is a heavenly task given of God. This fact is clear to everyone for many reasons, but principally on account of the venerable icon "made without hands", on which Jesus Christ, God made man, impressed his sacred face and sent it to Abgar the governor of Edessa, imprinted upon the holy veil. That it appeared a most beautiful and admirable work to his most chaste mother is known to all; she prayed for the apostle and evangelist Saint Luke, and blessed him on account of this profession, saying "May the grace of him who is born of me through me [be imparted] to them." Not only in this way, but it is also shown by the infinite miracles achieved and accomplished by the holy icons of the main feasts and those of the Virgin and the other saints, that the art of painting is acceptable and pleasing to God. Furthermore, those who do this work with devotion and diligence receive grace and blessing from God.'[1]

The two traditions to which Dionysius alludes — about King Abgar, and about St Luke as a painter — may well not be taken literally by Western Christians, but they form part of the background to iconography which is taken for granted by many, if not most, Orthodox Christians. These are traditions which enshrine important theological truths which need to be recognized as lying behind the great heritage of Orthodox icons and iconography.

The first tradition, about the icon known as 'The Saviour Acheiropoietos' — the icon of the Saviour 'made without hands' — goes back to the fifth century. This icon of the Holy Face of Christ, according to the legend, derives from an image of Christ's face which he miraculously caused to appear on a piece of cloth and sent to the envoys of King Abgar of Edessa as a means whereby the king would be healed. From the sixth century icons of the Holy Face were popular in Byzantium, but increasingly so after the transfer of the Edessa icon to Constantinople in 944. This icon is of great importance as a major focal point for Orthodox dogmatic teaching, in which the True Icon of God is Christ himself, the Incarnate Word and perfect Image of God. The image which is believed to have been given by Christ for the healing of King Abgar is likewise a gift not made by human hands, but by the very imprint of the Holy Face of the Redeemer. Thus, in this story the making of icons is linked to faith in the Incarnation of the Son of God; it is seen as part of the manifestation of the Incarnate Word, an unfolding of the mystery of God revealed in Christ. An icon is thus the servant of the Holy Tradition of the Church, a servant of the Gospel, not a mere artistic device. Just as the icon painter must be faithful to the delineation of the image of the Saviour made without hands, so the Church must be faithful to the Revelation given in and through him who is the True Icon of the invisible God.

Another important implication of the tradition of the icon

Acheiropoietos concerns the reason why it was sent to King Abgar. The image of the Holy Face of Christ was sent in order that the King might be healed of his disease; in the absence of Christ Himself, the Holy Image was to have the power to effect the healing of the king. The legend is saying virtually the same as St Paul in 2 Cor. 3.18:

> 'We all, with unveiled face, beholding the glory of the Lord, are being changed into his likeness from one degree of glory to another; for this comes from the Lord who is the Spirit.'

Beholding the glory of the Lord in worship, prayer and adoration, we are changed and transfigured by the presence of Christ; in the holy icons we come before the presence of Christ, and in them we too can find our healing and the restoration of the image of God in us. King Abgar and his leprosy can readily be seen to symbolize man's need for healing and restoration. That restoration is given in Christ, the perfect image of God and Man.

The tradition of the icon of the Saviour Acheiropoietos enshrines important truths about the relationship of revelation and icon painting; the second tradition to which Dionysius of Fourna alluded in the passage quoted above — that St Luke was the first person to paint icons of the Blessed Virgin Mary — enshrines other important truths about iconography and the Christian life. According to this tradition, St Luke painted his icons within the context of the work of the Holy Spirit within the Church; it is part of that revealing of the things of Christ which He promised would be done by the Spirit (John 16.13–15). The Church exists in the world as the body of Christ, the means of His continuing presence. The Church lives and works in the power of the Holy Spirit poured out at Pentecost, and its evangelical work is accomplished through word and image. St Luke the evangelist and iconographer symbolizes that continuing twofold aspect of the revelation of the Incarnate Son to the world.

These two traditions about the earliest icons teach us important truths about the place of icons in the life of the Church. First it is a part of that process whereby the Holy

Spirit leads us into the truth of Christ; this is not a matter that can be solely apprehended by the intellect in the Western sense, but truth that leads to the healing and restoration of man in the image of God. Second icons are as much a medium of revelation as the spoken or printed word; the grace and truth of God can enter our souls as much via the eye as via the ear; and the icon is therefore an important door through which we can enter into the world of the Spirit.

II

As the Church moved out from the Holy Land into the wider arena of the Mediterranean world, words and images together formed the language of communication by which the Gospel was passed on to others; the words, ideas and imagery current at that time in different parts of the civilized world were harnessed to form part of the Christian tradition, and to be the means whereby the experience of God's presence in Christ could be shared. The development of Christian art was to become an integral part of the Church's faith, teaching and worship, and the icons of the Orthodox Churches form one particular aspect of this development. However, it was not a process that was unopposed. In some parts of the Church there was considerable hostility to the visual arts late into the fourth century; anxieties and scruples about idolatry were felt by many Christians; St Basil the Great and St Gregory of Nyssa in the fourth century were the earliest major theologians to make positive statements about images. Yet in spite of recurring reservations and suspicions about images, the process of using contemporary ways of thought and artistic expression to convey the significance of Christian experience and faith continued to develop.

There is very little evidence of Christian painting or sculpture in the earliest years of the Church's existence. Around the year AD 250 the use of paintings in Christian buildings or burial places becomes more evident, and seems to have been developing at about the same time in various places throughout the Roman Empire; it seems that Christians in many places felt the need for external visual imagery alongside their verbal tradition, and in this development they made use of the visual 'lingua franca' of the Graeco-Roman culture of the day. The first Christian art is an adaptation of themes, images and motifs that were common in other religions and in the imperial art of the time. The fact that many of these images were adapted to themes in Christian teaching was central to the development of Christian art. When the Christian Church found itself — following the conversion of Constantine early in the fourth century — as the official religious body of the Roman Empire this process accelerated.

To appreciate some of the variety of Christian art and its different functions in the period up to the end of the fourth century, we must turn our attention to some of the elements that made up the non-Christian visual 'lingua franca', the earliest examples of Christian art, and then the way the function of this art changed with the conversion of Constantine and the establishment of 'Peace of the Church'.

Three images in particular are adapted to Christian use. The image of the shepherd with a lamb on his shoulders or standing amid his flock was common in Roman pagan art as a symbol of philanthropy; this was easily absorbed into the Christian tradition as a symbol of Christ the Good Shepherd, in whose care the faithful could rest secure, both in this life and in the life to come. A figure standing with hands raised in prayer was a common Roman symbol of piety; these 'orant' or praying figures soon found their place in Christian art to represent the attitude of mind in the faithful departed, or the actual person of the departed; later this figure was used to represent the Mother of God as a symbol of the praying Church. A third common figure was the philosopher, seated, with a scroll in one hand. Sometimes this was used to represent the wisdom of the departed believer; more frequently it was used to represent Christ as the true philosopher and source of Holy Wisdom, and his apostles as mediators of that Wisdom. In these three images — symbolizing the virtues of philanthropy, piety, and wisdom — we can see how biblical ideas could easily be expressed through the pagan traditions of the plastic arts. In painting and sculpture Christian artists used the visual language of the non-Christian world to express for the faithful the truths of Christianity.

In the New Testament the figure of the athlete striving to win the prize is used as an image of the Christian life (1 Cor. 9.24,25; Heb. 12.1–2; 2 Cor, 2.14), and one can see how easily this secular imagery of the Roman games is taken up into the language of Christian spirituality. The achievements of the successful gladiators and athletes become symbols of the glory that is the goal of the Christian life. Some scholars claim that there is evidence that these ideas found visual expression in early Christian funerary art, forming another cluster of ideas where secular imagery was at hand to create visual parallels. Yet another similar development took place after the conversion of the Emperor Constantine, when the imagery of imperial authority came to have a major influence on the art of the Christian Church.

In these examples we can see something of the intricate development of a Christian visual language which later blossomed out into great works of art; the development involved the interaction of biblical verbal imagery and pagan visual imagery, but the incentive behind the development lay in the spiritual needs of the faithful and the liturgical life of the Church. Two places, hundreds of miles apart, provide different sorts of examples of the developing Christian art in the third century.

In Rome, the catacombs used for Christian burial are very extensive; the paintings found there are frequently 'image-signs' which suggest events and their implications without fully representing them. These image-signs signify events in which the power of God to deliver the faithful has been demonstrated; for example, Daniel among the lions, Noah in the ark, Jonah being delivered from the belly of the whale, and Lazarus being raised from the dead. The dead have been buried in the faith that the God who delivered his people in the past will even now deliver them from death into life beyond the grave. These image-signs reflect the readings used and incidents referred to in the course of the burial rite. There are also symbols of even greater brevity: loaves and fishes to indicate the sacrament of the Eucharist and scenes of communal meals to indicate the multiplication of the loaves, or the Last Supper, or the heavenly banquet. Fish represents the soul immersed in the baptismal life, while fishermen indicate Christ and his apostles, the fishers of souls.

Far distant from Rome, on the eastern edge of the Empire was the town of Dura-Europos, which was conquered by the Parthians in 256. Part of the Roman defence of the town involved the burial of buildings that were adjacent to the city walls to provide reinforcements in the face of the Parthian attack from the east. Excavation on this site after the First World War revealed not only a building set aside for Christian worship, but also a Jewish synagogue. The synagogue had murals illustrating biblical material that pointed to God's power to save his people; such Jewish iconography was unknown before this excavation, but it indicates that some Jewish leaders no less than Christians felt the need to use the visual arts for the edification of their faithful in the midst of an alien culture. The baptistery of the church building in Dura-Europos is dominated by a mural of the Good Shepherd who dwarfs the figures of Adam and Eve; this powerfully represents the dogmas of original sin, Christ's work of redemption, and our entry into the flock of Christ through the waters of Baptism. Other murals show scenes relating to the use of water in Baptism and the new life in Christ conferred through this sacrament.

In the art of the catacombs and of the church at Dura-Europos there is a liturgical setting and a concern for the salvation of the individual; in connection with both baptism and burial the iconography points to the gift of salvation in and through the Christian Church. After the conversion of Constantine there is a rapid increase in the extent of church building and of Christian art; its quality improves as official resources are devoted to the propagation of the Christian religion, and the visual arts are harnessed to serve the teaching needs of the Church. The sheer pressure of numbers of people coming into the life of the Church meant that the visual arts could now be publicly and extensively employed in the service of teaching and liturgical worship; paintings on the walls of churches and baptistries often represented passages from the Old Testament and the Gospels that were read in church or incidents that were alluded to in the course of the liturgy. Iconography thus became less concerned with the symbolism of salvation for those whose Christian commitment could lead to persecution, and more concerned to instruct and edify those who have been baptized. Thus Orthodox Christian art came to be as it is now, closely inter-related to the liturgy and spirituality of the Church. It is never a separate affair; Orthodox church art never exists for its own sake. The language of iconography, like the language of the Scriptures and the dogma of the Church, is part of the language of the Church's spiritual tradition; it is there to open up and deepen man's spiritual perception, and lead him further into the life of worship and adoration.

III

By the early years of the fourth century the Christian Church had experienced times of tolerance by the Roman authorities and times of intense persecution. For the first 300 years of its existence the Christian Church was a minority group with a faith that often provoked enmity from the State. Sometimes Christians formed convenient scapegoats who could be blamed for problems in Roman society and then killed; at other times, the Christians' refusal to accept the divinity of an Emperor was a common reason for persecution. 'The blood of the martyrs is the seed of the Church', was a comment by Tertullian (d. 220) which summed up the sacrifice and suffering which many early Christians had to endure. 'The Church of the martyrs' was a tried and tested body of people, a spiritual elite who had been schooled in days of persecution; the symbolic death of Baptism brought them into the New Life of Christ, but physical death at the hands of the Roman authorities was a risk that had to be accepted as a consequence of Baptism.

This situation changed radically with the Edict of Toleration issued by the Emperor Constantine at Milan in 313. The Church acquired civil status and the same privileges as the religious institutions of the State. Constantine inaugurated the Christianization of the Roman Empire; he became sole Emperor in 324, uniting Eastern and Western halves of the Empire again under one authority. And in 330 his new capital at the ancient Greek city of Byzantium on the Bosphorus was dedicated as Constantinople, the New Rome. Byzantium gave its name to an Empire that lasted for over a thousand years until Constantinople was destroyed in 1453. To many people in the West the Byzantine Empire is largely unknown, rarely figuring in history books except in connection with the Crusades and the final overthrow of Constantinople. Yet Constantine's foundation of the New Rome led to an Empire in many ways as vibrant and glorious as that of the first Rome; it was an Empire based on the faith that God had raised up Constantine to fulfil His purposes, and entrusted to the new Rome the faith that the old Rome had so long failed to accept. The Imperial Court of Byzantium came to be seen as the earthly counterpart of the Heavenly Court.

But the Edict of Toleration, while signalling the end of the Church of the Martyrs, brought new problems for the Church. It was no longer the spiritual elite prepared for any eventuality. 'An incalculable shoal of good and bad fishes had been caught up in the nets of the Church' was how St Augustine described the influx of new members when the risk of persecution had been removed. Conflicts about the faith had hitherto been solved by the Church without outside interference; now however, the Emperor's concern for unity of faith throughout the Empire meant that conflict within the Church was a matter for imperial intervention. The first Ecumenical Council at Nicea took place in 325, only one year after Constantine became sole Emperor; Constantine's initiative in convoking the council in order to settle the Arian conflict left a pattern for his successors to follow, but the bishops and leaders of the Church were not easily manipulated, and many a bishop went into exile rather than compromise his conscience and faith under pressure from an emperor. In fact on some occasions it was bishops who put pressure on emperors, as when St Ambrose of Milan insisted that the Emperor Theodosius do penance before receiving the sacrament after his soldiers had committed mass murder in the amphitheatre at Thessalonica.

Following from the profound changes brought into the life of the Church by the Edict of Toleration, there was a great development of Christian monasticism. It was a new form of witness (Greek: *martus*) after the witness of martyrdom had ceased to be the price one might have to pay for one's faith. The 'shoal of good and bad fishes' that entered the life of the Church after the Edict of Toleration included many who found it expedient to belong to the Church, and who were in no way committed to a rigorous Christian discipleship. It was partly as a response to such time-serving new members that the monastic movement developed, rejecting the values and assumptions of Roman society in order to preserve the purity of Christian commitment. From Egypt monasticism spread throughout the Eastern provinces of the Empire and then into the West; the great spiritual leaders of the Church were often drawn from the monasteries, and by the late fourth century some of the greatest bishops and theologians were those whose main spiritual formation had been in the monastic life.

In the new climate of toleration, Christian art flourished, and it was the capital, Constantinople, that was the scene of many of the most important developments. From this period imperial imagery begins to be increasingly used in Christian art, with Christ shown enthroned as ruler of the universe, and the Virgin also enthroned and sharing in the glory of heaven. It is to this period also that we can trace the origins of the later ideal of the Byzantine Christian Imperial Court as the earthly counterpart of the Heavenly Court; coins and medals of this period begin to show the Emperor seated in majesty beneath the Hand of God, the Christian Emperor entrusted with a divine responsibility and authority. The height of artistic achievement in the Byzantine Empire's early centuries was reached in the reign of the Emperor Justinian from 527 to 565. Justinian pursued the vision of a restored Roman Empire with great energy and resolve, recapturing much territory in the West that had been previously lost to Vandals and Goths who had invaded the Western Empire in the fifth century. In matters of religion he sought to enforce unity throughout the

Empire in the face of heretical divisions in Egypt and Syria; he codified the traditions of Roman Law in a way that formed the basic legal system for the whole of the duration of the Byzantine Empire, and that passed into western society in the eleventh century. Vast patronage was also channelled into cultural and artistic work for the glory of both Church and State.

Justinian's greatest creation was the church of Hagia Sophia in Constantinople; this — the most important and impressive church in the Empire — was begun in February 532 and completed in December 537. The architects, Anthemius of Tralles and Isodorus of Miletus, supervised one hundred master builders and ten thousand labourers, using the finest and rarest materials from many parts of the Empire. The imaginative and daring design, the relentless labour, and the massive imperial expenditure all resulted in one of the most outstanding buildings in the history of Christendom. A contemporary writer, Procopius, who had no great love or respect for the Emperor, was unstinting in his praise of the interior of the restored Hagia Sophia:

> 'The church has become a spectacle of marvellous beauty, overwhelming to those who see it, but to those who know it by hearsay altogether incredible . . . And it exults in an indescribable beauty. For it proudly reveals its mass and the harmony of its proportions, having neither any excess nor deficiency, since it is both more preventious than the buildings to which we are accustomed, and considerably more noble than those which are merely huge, and it abounds exceedingly in sunlight and in the reflection of the sun's rays from the marble. Indeed one might say that its interior is not illuminated from without by the sun, but that the radiance comes into being within it, such an abundance of light bathes this shrine . . . The upper part of this structure . . . seems somehow to float in the air on no firm basis, but to be poised aloft to the peril of those inside it. Yet actually it is braced with exceptional firmness and security.
>
> All these details . . . produce a single and most extraordinary harmony in the work, and yet do not permit the spectator to linger much over the study of any one of them, but each

detail attracts the eye and draws it on irresistibly to itself . . . Observers are unable to understand the skilful craftsmanship, but they always depart from there overwhelmed by the bewildering sight.

And whenever anyone enters this church to pray, he understands at once that it is not by any human power or skill, but by the influence on God, that this work has been so finely turned. And so his mind is lifted up toward God and exalted, feeling that He cannot be far away, but must especially love to dwell in this place which He has chosen.'[2]

As Justinian entered the completed building it is said he cried out 'Solomon, I have triumphed over you!'.

IV

By the time of Justinian it was accepted that iconography was to be used as a servant of the Christian faith. Great theologians of an earlier generation had acknowledged that the visual work of artists could communicate with greater immediacy than the written or spoken word. At the end of a long oration in honour of the martyr St Barlaam, St Basil, one of the fourth century Fathers of the Church, appeals to the painters to complete his commemoration:

'Complete with your art this incomplete image of a great leader. Illuminate with the flowers of your wisdom the indistinct image which I have drawn of the crowned martyr. Let my words be surpassed by your painting of the heroic deeds of the martyr . . . and I will look at this fighter represented in a more living way on your paintings'.[3]

Similarly, St Gregory of Nyssa, another of the fourth century Fathers, says 'The silent painting speaks on the walls and does much good'.[4]

The artistic means which had been used to promote the imperial ideologies in the days before Constantine were now used to promote Orthodoxy in the face of heresy. Although the earliest developments of Christian art had been 'unofficial', and had occurred in diverse parts of the Empire, once the

Imperial concern for unity within the Empire was linked with the Church's concern for the unity of the Orthodox faith throughout Christendom, 'official' considerations had a major influence on Christian art. The addition of the Greek letters Alpha and Omega to icons of Christ stressed His divinity, thus upholding the teaching of the Council of Nicea. The decisions of the Council of Ephesus in 431 which condemned the heretical teaching of Nestorius had an influence on the way the Virgin and Child were represented in iconography; the emphasis was on Mary as Theotokos, God-bearer, and on the divine nature of the Child she holds.

The stability of the Byzantine Empire was seriously disturbed during the seventh century by the rise of Islam — a new religion with a political impact that shook the whole of the eastern Mediterranean world. The Moslems conquered Syria, Iraq, Egypt and Persia; the Christian holy places in and near Jerusalem fell into Moslem hands, and Constantinople itself was attacked. The attacks on the Empire created a serious crisis in which many Christians were perplexed by the success of this new religion — a religion with no images, with a strong prohibition of idolatry, and a powerful assertion of the sovereignty of the one God. The Emperor Leo III in 717 conquered the Arabs who were besieging Constantinople, and he began a reign of twenty four years in which he sought to reform and consolidate what remained of the Empire, and to purge the Church of its images. This policy of Leo III had profound effects on the Church; his action precipitated what has come to be known as the Iconoclast Controversy — a conflict which centered on the place of visual representation in relation to the Christian faith, and the nature of authority within the Church and the Empire. It was a conflict that lasted from about 726 to 843, with a period of respite from 787 to 815.

By the time the Iconoclast controversy began, the range of Christian representational art was quite considerable: it included the didactic, illustrative material used in churches; the images of Christ and the Virgin that had an official, dogmatic function; the motifs and images that were related to Christian burial; and it also included a range of images of saints (St Meletius and St Simeon Stylites were particularly popular in Antioch) that were often taken away from a liturgical setting and used in homes and shops, and given a degree of veneration that was not purely commemorative. The extent of the veneration of images caused considerable anxiety and concern to some Christian leaders, partly because of Old Testament prohibitions of idolatry (which contemporary Jewish leaders were taking particularly seriously), and partly because of the emergence of the powerful Islamic faith with its insistence on simplicity and the unity of God. Also, various parts of the Church still suffered from docetic tendencies, which denied the true humanity of Christ and the reality of the Incarnation, thus standing out against the mainstream of Orthodox teaching as determined by the Ecumenical Councils. Between 726 and 730 the Emperor Leo III promoted decrees in the Senate which set off the conflict between the Iconodules (literally 'icon-worshippers') and Iconoclasts (destroyers of icons). Vast numbers of images, whether painted, sculptured, in mosaic or in textiles, were brutally destroyed, and a period of ecclesiastical vandalism set in throughout most of the Empire, as it had now become official Imperial ideology to destroy the icons. This Imperial ideology as it related to the Church was an intrusion into the faith and affairs of the Church; it was not only externals, but the Orthodox faith itself that was being attacked. It is this attack on the autonomy and faith of the Church, as well as the attack on the holy icons, that elicited such courageous and heroic resistance by the defenders of the icons: their loyalty was not just to holy icons, but to the faith of the Church as determined by holy tradition and the Ecumenical Councils.

The savagery of the destruction of icons during the Iconoclast period has meant that very few icons remain from the period before 726. Those that did survive were later found mainly in remote monasteries which escaped the zeal of the iconoclasts; others were in remote monasteries outside the Empire. Egypt and Syria had been lost by the Empire to the rising tide of Islam in the seventh century, and although some of the Islamic leaders ordered the removal of icons from Christian churches in their territory, it was not a policy that was consistently enacted. Thus the very remote monastery of St Catherine on Mount Sinai is the main source of icons from before 726; as an imperial foundation it had many icons from the best workshops in Constantinople, as well as from other sources, and it is these early icons from the sixth and seventh centuries which are the prime examples of iconography before the storm of iconoclasm broke out in 726.

Chapter Three

HISTORICAL BACKGROUND
The Triumph of Orthodoxy and later developments

I

On the death of the Emperor Theophilus in 842 his widow Theodora — of the Orthodox or Icondule party — became regent for his son Michael III, and the persecution of the icondules ceased. In 843 a Council held in Constantinople under Patriarch St Methodius re-established the veneration of the holy icons in terms which had been defined in 787 at the seventh Ecumenical Council which took place at the beginning of the respite in the controversy referred to earlier.

Now the feast of the Triumph of Orthodoxy was established, to be celebrated on the first Sunday in Lent, and sacred art once against assumed a prominent place in the life of the Orthodox Churches. But things could not, of course, simply return to the state of affairs that had prevailed before 726. The ferocity of the conflict had led to many new martyrs; lives had been sacrificed to the truth of Orthodoxy and the use of the holy icons; the conflict of ideas had led the defenders of the icons to a much more thoroughly developed defence of icons and their veneration. After 843, public devotion to icons was resumed with a much more self-conscious theological basis than before; the icons were to have a much more profoundly worked out religious function beyond that of illustration and teaching.

During the conflict the two most prominent theologians who wrote in defence of the holy icons were St John of Damascus (c.675 – c.749) and St Theodore of Studios (759 – 826). These developed the theological defence and veneration of the icons, not as matters separate from the mainstream of

Orthodox theology, but as issues which were inextricably bound up with the doctrine of Creation and the Incarnation. From their works we can see four specific issues that have had continuing significance for the Christian view of the world we live in and its relationship with its Creator.

The first issue was the place of matter in God's scheme of things. How matter was to be perceived and used became an issue of great controversy during the Iconoclast period. If paint and pigment were 'mere matter', then any veneration shown to the icons could be interpreted as idolatry — the giving to a creature of that worship and honour that are due to God alone. The arguments of the time were complex, but the theological position which was reached in the seventh Ecumenical Council was that the use of icons was not idolatrous, and was essentially in keeping with the doctrines of Creation and Incarnation. Many people of that time saw matter and spirit in terms of a scale of being in which matter was very near the bottom end of the scale, a long, long way from the spiritual level of the Godhead. The Church's Creeds and Councils had asserted the faith that the second Person of the Holy Trinity had actually entered into the world of matter, taken our human flesh and blood, and raised our humanity into the life of the Godhead: 'The Word made flesh has deified the flesh' (St John of Damascus). Thus any idea of an unbridgable gap between God and man could not be tolerated; nor could ideas that matter was the work of the devil. Matter, in the Christian view, is the work of the Divine artist, and as such mediates divine grace. Man is restored in Christ to share in the creative work of the Divine artist as the priest of creation, being the mediator between the material world and the creator.

> 'Through heaven and earth and sea, through wood and stone, through relics and church buildings and the Cross, through angels and men, through all creation visible and invisible, I offer veneration and honour to the Creator and Master and Maker of all things, and to him alone. For the creation does not venerate the Maker directly and by itself, but it is through me that the heavens declare the glory of God, through me the moon worships God, through me the stars glorify him, through

me the waters and showers of rain, the dew and all creation, venerate God and give him glory.'

Leontius of Cyprus (seventh century)[1]

Second, the reality of the Incarnation was at stake. If the argument about icons was based on Old Testament prohibitions it was failing to recognize the nature of the revelation that had been given since those prohibitions. The Mosaic commandment had been given 'before the age of grace . . . when God had not yet been revealed in the flesh'[2] (Theodore of Studios). To argue against icons on the basis of the Old Testament was to ignore the fact that the Son of God had come in the flesh and restored the image of God in man.

Nor was the argument in favour of mental contemplation alone acceptable to Theodore:

> 'If merely mental contemplation were sufficient, it would have been sufficient for Him to come to us in a merely mental way.'[3]

In Orthodoxy, theology and art, word and image, are seen as two aspects of the one Revelation. Those who defended the veneration of the Holy Icons in the troubled times of the eighth and ninth centuries believed they were fighting for the truth of the Incarnation of the Son of God; and they believed that those who attacked the icons were attacking the reality of the Incarnation and the possibility of that revelation being communicated through matter.

Third, the defenders of the icons were defending a view of revelation that worked through sight as well as sound, through the eye as well as the ear. Since God had been revealed in the flesh, matter and art as well as word were the means the Spirit used to continue the work of revelation. Theodore argued that both hearing and sight are essential for a full assimilation of what God has revealed in Christ. According to Theodore, Christ . . .

> 'nowhere told anyone to write down the "concise word"; yet his image was drawn in writing by the apostles and has been preserved up to the present. Whatever is marked there with paper and ink, the same is marked on the icon with various pigments or some other material. For the great Basil says:

"Whatever the words of the narrative offer, the picture silently shows by imitation"'.[4]

And in another place he adds:

'Hearing is equal to sight, and it is necessary to use both senses'.[5]

The seventh Ecumenical Council put that same view:

'Iconography was not at all invented by painters, but on the contrary, it is an approved institution and a tradition of the Catholic Church. That which the word communictes by sound, the painting demonstrates silently by representation.'[6]

The language of sacred art is thus a language that corresponds to that of the sacred writings. It is not simply a matter of art illustrating the words of Scripture.

The fourth issue was the veneration of icons. The defenders of the holy icons asserted that these images were distinct from the originals they represented — Christ, the Saints, events in the Gospels — but that they merited relative veneration and honour, different from the worship that is reserved for God alone. Such veneration as was paid to an icon was directed not to the paint and pigment, but to the reality represented in the paint and pigment. Thus, Theodore of Studios writes:

'Christ is depicted in images, and the invisible is seen. He who in His own divinity is uncircumscribable accepts the circumscription natural to His Body. The veneration of the image is the veneration of Christ. The material of the image is not venerated at all, but only Christ who has his likeness in it.'[7]

And St John of Damascus writes:

'I do not adore matter, but I adore the Creator of matter, who became matter for me, inhabiting matter and accomplishing my salvation through matter.'[8]

To this day the·Orthodox Churches maintain a strict distinction between the worship that is offered to God alone, and the veneration or reverence that is paid to the holy icons. This preserves the insight that the icon is not an idol, but a symbol by means of which contact is made with a more profound relity. We must look upon icons as doors or windows through which we are open to the sanctifying grace of the Spirit, a meeting point of man and God, continuing the work of the Incarnation in a way that combines with the Scriptures to lead man into the Divine Life of the Blessed Trinity.

The faith for which St John of Damascus and St Theodore of Studios fought is stated in a slightly different way a thousand years later by Dionysius of Fourna in his *Painter's Manual*:

'The painting of holy images we take over not only from the holy fathers, but also from the holy apostles and even from the very person of Christ our only God . . . We therefore depict Christ on an icon as a man, since he came into the world and had dealings with men, becoming in the end a man like us, except in sin.

We also represent the image of the Virgin and of all the saints, according them worship* indirectly, not to the image itself; that is to say we do not say that this really is Christ, or the Virgin, or whichever saint it is that is represented on the icon, but the honour that we pay to the icon we accord to the prototype, that is to say to the person who is shown to us on the icon. Since we give a different degree of worship to the icon of Christ and kiss it, the honour which we pay it we really make to Christ himself, the son of God, seated on the right hand of the throne of the greatness on high, who for us became man.

We do not worship the colours and the skill, as those who are opposed to our Church clearly blaspheme, the faithless and the heretics, but we worship our Lord Jesus Christ, who is in heaven; for as Basil says, the honour paid to the icon passes on to the prototype.

We say the same things concerning the icons of all the saints, since seeing one martyr painted we are immediately reminded that this saint was a man like us. Thus with all of them through his endurance he overcame tyrants and disclosed idolatry, affirming the faith of Christ with his blood.

Again, seeing one of the bishops, we think that this same man with his virtuous policy became a fine example to his

*The translation used here is Paul Hetherington's; I would, however, prefer the word 'veneration' to 'worship'.

flock, and guided them into the pastures of safety, and with the wisdom of his words drove away the heretics from the Church of Christ. Again, seeing a holy man, we think that he with his exercises overcame the snares of the devil, keeping his body pure and living a holy life. And we say, simply seeing any saint depicted on an icon, that we immediately recall his works and worship him and praise him, projecting our minds up to the prototype, giving thanks to God who made them possible and won so many contests, and strengthened Orthodoxy.'[9]

II

After the Triumph of Orthodoxy the place of icons in the life of the Orthodox Church was secure; they were an integral part of the setting of worship, and integrated into the faith of Orthodoxy itself. Throughout the Byzantine world churches were decorated with similar iconographic schemes, whether they were executed as mosaics, frescoes, or painted wood-panel icons. Styles varied in different parts of the Empire, and at different stages in history, but essentially it was the art of the Church which was being created, an art that was the servant of the faith and the liturgy, and that played an essential part in the communication between the divine and human realms.

The history of the Byzantine Empire was constantly marked by external pressures on its frontiers; the extent of the Empire was rarely static, because of the constant attacks to which it was subjected. From the North came recurring waves of Goths, Slavs and Bulgars; from the East and South came the Persians, the Muslim forces, and the Turkish invaders, the latter being responsible for the final conquest of Constantinople in 1453; and from the West came the Normans. A great expansion of the Empire under the Macedonian dynasty (867 – 1056) was followed by a period of contraction and severe economic problems in the Comnene dynasty (1081 – 1185); in 1204 the imperial power of Byzantium collapsed under the attack of the forces of the Fourth Crusade — a supposedly Christian expedition — and the period of Latin rule in Constantinople began. This came to an end in 1261 when the capital was recovered by Michael VIII Palaeologus, and the Palaeologan dynasty continued until the ultimate collapse of 1453.

In the three main periods of history measured by these imperial dynasties we can recognize distinctive characteristics in Orthodox Church art. In the Macedonian period the inspiration from the Classical period is very strong; dignity, nobility and a rather monumental character epitomize the mosaics and frescoes of this time. During the Comnene period there was a considerable revival in the arts, in spite of the dire economic and social problems of the time. The revival of spirituality under the influence of people like St Symeon the New Theologian (949 – 1022) had a direct influence on the art of this period; stylized, heiratic forms became more common; there was a greater emphasis on 'dematerializing' the bodies of the figures represented in frescoes; a greater intimacy develops in the figures and a high degree of spirituality. During the Crusader period of rule in Constantinople (1204 – 61) there was considerable interaction between Western and Eastern artistic traditions in the areas under Latin control, whilst in Asia Minor in the Empires of Nicea and Trebizond the purer Byzantine traditions were maintained. With the restoration of the Byzantine Empire under the Palaeologues another great resurgence of artistic activity took place, epitomized by frescoes and icons of great humanity and vitality. *(See plate 18)*

Just as the frontiers of the Empire were broken through by attack from outside they were also the starting-point for considerable missionary expansion on the part of the Byzantines. Although the Orthodox Church's influence at the western edge of the Empire ebbed and flowed with the political developments there, to the north extensive and highly effective missionary work was undertaken among the Bulgarians and the Slavs. Most important in this was the work of the two brothers St Cyril and St Methodius in the late ninth century. To further the mission of the Church, St Cyril invented the 'Glagolithic' alphabet and translated the liturgy and the Scriptures into Slavonic (The Orthodox Churches have always allowed the liturgy to be celebrated in the vernacular language of any country where they have taken root). The Cyrillic script (often inaccurately attributed to St Cyril himself) was invented about the same time and passed into general use in the new Slavonic Churches. The missionary work that was to have particular long-term significance, however, was that which took place after the conversion of Prince Vladimir of Kiev in 988. What was to emerge from this was a major new section of the Orthodox Church that was intimately linked with Byzantium, but politically independent; the language of the Russian Church was Slavonic, but its faith and practice were in harmony with Constantinople.

Constantinople was the nerve-centre for Orthodoxy as well as the capital of the Byzantine Empire. The Byzantine world was a sacral one, where spiritual and secular energies were thought to function in harmony with each other; the rituals of the Imperial Court and the liturgy of the Church each reflected something of the God-given order of creation itself, a heirarchical universe in which each part had its own particular function to fulfil. The balance and order were not always maintained, but such failures did not negate the value and power of the ideals.

The conversion of the Slavs was a major move by the Orthodox Church into an area beyond the Empire where spiritual and commercial links were maintained with Constantinople. As the Church spread further into Northern and Eastern Russia through the activities of individual monks and communities it was the same Orthodox faith that was taken. However far away from Kiev and Constantinople they spread, these missionaries were part of the one Church, and were nourished spiritually by movements in Byzantium that spread their influence through the trade routes linking the Baltic and Black Seas. It is this continuity of communication between Russia and Byzantium, and their sense of being parts of the same church, that accounts for the close spiritual inter-relationship that existed between monastic communities in Russia and the Eastern Mediterranean world. For example, the founder of monasticism in Kievan Russia, St Anthony of Kiev (983 – 1073), according to legend, was professed at the monastery of Esphigmenou, on Mount Athos (a peninsula jutting out from the Greek mainland which for centuries has been home for monastic communities from all the various parts of the Orthodox world). The Studite monastic rule was taken from Constantinople to St Theodosius of Kiev (1035 – 1074), one of the pupils of St Anthony. In the thirteenth century there were continuing links between Church leaders in Novgorod and Kiev with Constantinople and Athos, and during the time prior to the fall of Constantinople the Hesychast movement associated with St Gregory Palamas (c.1296 – c.1359) had a profound influence in Russia, particularly through St Sergius and his disciples.

III

When in 1453 the Turkish Sultan Mehmet II finally conquered Constantinople and the last Byzantine Emperor Constantine XI Palaeologus was killed in the fighting, Moscow had been the centre of the Orthodox Church in Russia for a century and a quarter. In order to help us understand the broad outlines of the development of the history of the Russian State and Church we might look briefly at the celebrated icon of Our Lady of Vladimir. This work which has become one of the best known symbols of the whole Russian spiritual tradition was probably painted in Constantinople in about 1130. From the mother city it came to Russia as part of the Orthodox faith. Since first being taken to Kiev just after it was painted, it was transferred to Vyshegorod, then in 1185 to Vladimir, and finally in 1395 to Moscow. Its movements through Russia reflected the vicissitudes of Russian history, and the different stages in the emergence of the Russian state. The Kievan state spanning the main routes from the Baltic to the Black Sea and including such important centres as Novgorod, Pskov, Rostov and Suzdal, disintegrated before the end of the twelfth century. For nearly 200 years Russia was a group of fragmented principalities continually threatened by Mongol incursions from the East; the ending of the Mongol occupation with Dimitry Donskoy's victory over the Mongols at the Battle of Kulikovo Polye in 1380 was a major turning point, but it still left a collection of smaller principalities and city states jealously guarding their own independence. During this time there was immense spiritual activity taking place particularly through the work and inspiration of St Sergius of Radonezh (1314 – 92) and his disciples; the pattern of retreat to the hermit life, the growth of monastic communities, and the development of wider community life in the remoter fringes of Russian territory was repeated many times in the lives of great Russian saints. Monasticism and missionary activity were all intertwined, and in this pattern of Russian Christianity the artistic traditions of Byzantine Orthodoxy were assimilated and developed.

The painting of frescoes and wooden panel icons flourished throughout Russia, with centres like Novgorod and Pskov being very prolific before the rise of the city which was to dominate them all — Moscow. A new peak of icon painting was reached in the fifteenth century which was directly linked to the hesychast movement in Byzantium and the work of St Sergius and his disciples in Russia in the mid to late fourteenth century; the new emphasis on the Divine Light permeating and transfiguring the created world through the practice of mystical prayer can be seen in the work of Andrei Rublev, the most famous being his Old Testament Trinity (1411); here inner luminosity permeates matter and brings to a new intensity the artistic and spiritual work of icon painters. Contemporary with Rublev was Theophanes the Greek whose work in the Moscow area is further evidence of the way the Greek artistic workshops helped to spread the traditions of spirituality that had their roots in the theological soil of Byzantium.

Before the end of the fifteenth century the Muscovite Russian state was set on a course of expansion that would lead to the annexation of the city state of Novgorod and other territories, the exaltation of Moscow as the spiritual and political centre of Russia, and the development of a Muscovite ideology whose consequences are still being worked out in the international arena of the twentieth century. The conquest of Byzantium by the Turks in 1453 occurred at the time Muscovy was expanding in political power, and had already assimilated into its life much of the ethos, culture, and spirituality of Byzantium. Very soon after the collapse of Constantinople, the 'Second Rome', Moscow was beginning to be called the 'Third Rome', the new city and state entrusted with a divinely appointed mission. The Second Rome had failed its trust and been destroyed; the sacred fire of Orthodoxy was now entrusted to a new vessel, the Third Rome of the Muscovite Grand Princes. The title of Czar (Caesar) shows particularly vividly the link through Byzantium to the Roman Empire; rather less straightforward were the legends and mythologies that linked the Russian princes genealogically right back to Caesar Augustus. The Russian rulers came to be seen as custodians and saviours of Orthodoxy, the bearers of a divine mission which had been removed from the trust of the Byzantine world and transferred to Muscovy. The devotion with which this trust was taken up were no doubt very commendable, but what was notably lacking were the intellectual, theological and critical expertize that had been an essential part of the Byzantine tradition. The 'package' was transmitted complete; but it could not be maintained at its former level. The truth of Orthodoxy in all its parts was defended and promoted — there are many Russian saints who are examples of zeal and heroic sanctity — but there was in the Russian Church no degree of theological competence comparable to that found in the Byzantine world.

With the death of Byzantium, Holy Russia was born. The traditions of Rome and Constantinople passed to Moscow, and in many ways they still remain there, in spite of the changes wrought by the Russian Revolution.

IV

The long and complicated history of the Church under Turkish rule in the Mediterranean lands, and under the Czars cannot be dealt with in this book. The most important development of these centuries for the history of icons was the meeting of Orthodox art with that of post-Renaissance Western Europe. In Russia this came to a head at the time of Peter the Great (1672 – 1725), with his policy of opening up

Russia to the Western world; in his time and afterwards the influence of Western religious and secular art was promoted within Russia, with an emphasis on realism and a deliberate denigration of the authentic traditions of Orthodox iconography. In the Mediterranean world places like Northern Greece and Crete were, however, able to maintain the authentic traditions of icon painting well into the eighteenth century, sometimes with rather unusual mixtures of styles due to Venetian influence. In other places like the monastic centres of Mount Athos and the Meteora (another monastic centre in northern Greece), defensive zeal for the old traditions faced with increasing pressure to follow Western influence led to rather ossified forms and styles. As we have already seen, the *Painter's Manual* of Dionysius of Fourna is a valuable and nteresting witness to the faith and traditions of Orthodox icon painting, but it also betrays a lack of fresh inspiration and perhaps an overstated concern to defend the details of a tradition whose inner vitality has already been sapped. By the eighteenth century in Greece, as in Russia, those willing or rich enough to patronize the arts had already been seduced by the philosophy and art of the non-Orthodox world.

Within the Orthodox world icons continued to be painted; many in the nineteenth and twentieth centuries bear the hallmarks of the worst Western religious art; they represent sacred themes and are therefore duly accorded reverence and veneration, but they lack the spiritual power and intensity of the great works that belong to the older traditions of iconography. Fortunately these older works have been preserved, and, along with the spiritual tradition deep within Orthodoxy, still provide a stimulus to further development and renewal. In Greece and in other parts of the Orthodox Church there has been a considerable revival in the art of icon painting and in the spirituality that lies at the heart of Orthodoxy. This revival has caught the imagination and attention of many Western Christians, who have found in icons a way in to other aspects of the Orthodox faith. The doors of perception are not completely closed.

Chapter Four

BIBLICAL LANGUAGE
Verbal and visual imagery

I

The prohibition of the use of 'graven images' in Jewish worship in Old Testament times had a profound influence on the whole biblical tradition of theology and spirituality. God could not be represented in a visual form that was worthy of adoration and worship; however much God had made himself known to the people of Old Testament times, he was still a God who was hidden, beyond the grasp of mortal man's comprehension. Yet in the context of the New Testament this 'hidden' God made himself known in Jesus Christ. The God beyond the comprehension of man entered human life as Man; in the Incarnation God revealed himself, and also the true vocation of man, in the person of Jesus Christ. The invisible was made visible in the face of Jesus Christ. In him the image of God was perfectly revealed.

The way in which God's revelation of himself in both Old and New Testament times was perceived and expressed made use of a language that consisted of more than words. The language of theology and spirituality has to express that which is beyond the normal routine of human life and experience, yet still related to it; this language makes use of ordinary 'verbal' language, but also consists of a rich 'vocabulary' of symbols which enable us to speak of other dimensions to human life. The word 'symbol' derives from Greek words meaning 'to draw together'; (the opposite is 'diabolic', that which tears apart). Symbols allow us to draw together different perceptions, different levels of understanding and meaning, different dimensions to human experience; symbols become the focal point at which the material and the spiritual, the ordinary and the extra-ordinary, the human and the divine converge in human perception.

The Mosaic Law may have included the prohibition of the

worship of graven images, but it did not remove other sorts of imagery from the biblical tradition; indeed, the ban on graven images may well have been a stimulus to the development of a rich stock of verbal and poetic images, concepts, and ideas within the biblical tradition of theology and spirituality.

Part of the verbal imagery and symbolism of the Bible remains in the Christian tradition as words and verbal images, sometimes expressed in decorative art in churches. In this connection water, wine, bread, stone, rock, and fire are common examples in both Old and New Testaments. In the parables of Jesus we find mustard seed, wheat, yeast, lost coins and valuable pearls being used to express truths about the Kingdom of God; they remain verbal images and symbols of considerable power, but have rarely lent themselves to 'translation' into visual representation.

Other elements in biblical symbolism and imagery have a very powerful visual aspect, and have naturally found their way into the traditions of Christian art and icon painting. Light is a symbol of truth, goodness and revelation; it can be used in connection with a particular source or person. This can be conveyed by the quality of luminosity and illumination in an icon *(see plates 6, 13 and 16)*. Early in the Bible, in the book of Genesis, the tree of the knowledge of good and evil, and the tree of life, are part of the symbolic language of the Scriptures; this symbolism is used again at the end of the New Testament in the Book of Revelation, where the tree of life stands near the river of the water of life, and bears leaves that are for the healing of the nations: in many icons, a tree stands somewhere in the scene, and may be seen as a symbol of the life which God intends for his people *(see plate 4)*. Moses, Elijah and Jesus are often said to be on hills or mountains at particularly important points in their relationship with God; the mountain top has been taken as a symbol of closeness to God and the giving of revelation in those situations which are apart from the ordinary routine of human life: in icons mountains often form part of the background, or are sometimes reduced to a distorted symbol of a mountain, and we can see how the visual tradition of iconography picks up and develops the verbal imagery of the Bible *(see plates 4 and 6)*.

Another profound symbol in the Bible is that of the Temple, the meeting place of God and his people; it is a place that can be abused and defiled, cleansed and restored, or laid waste and destroyed; it remains a powerful symbol in the Book of Revelation. In icons of the events that take place in the Temple (e.g. the Presentation of the Virgin and of Christ — *see plate 11*) there is a strong sense that here is the meeting place of God and man, the focal point of some particular stage in the drama of redemption. In St John's Gospel, Christ speaks of himself as the door of the sheepfold, the means whereby we enter into the divine life; in the Book of Revelation the writer speaks of a door open in heaven, through which he is invited to pass in order to receive revelation. Although these two specific uses of the imagery of the door are not often 'translated' into visual representation in icons, many icons have a multitude of doors and windows in impossible positions in the architectural background to the central events portrayed; these are best understood as hints, reminders and symbols that in what is represented we are entering the world of the spirit, the world of divine revelation where the ordinary language of human communication is stretched to breaking point to describe the indescribable!

II

Some particular ideas and images used in the New Testament became key theological concepts in later Christian teaching and worship; they became part of the very structure of Christianity. Frequently they were ideas which became bones of contention between Christians and Jews, between spiritual and secular authorities, and between different traditions of thought and spirituality within the Church itself. As with the symbols discussed earlier, so with these more specifically Christian themes there is a varied potential for visual expression in icons; some ideas and themes easily 'translate' into a visual language, while others remain more verbal and cerebral.

'The Kingdom of God' is a key theme in the Gospels, and was central to the teaching of Jesus. God's sovereignty, rule

and authority are made present in Christ in a way that
challenges the secure and brings hope to the poor. By his
preaching and ministry Christ opens up the way to the
Kingdom of God, both as an inner reality in the hearts of his
hearers, and also as a reality whose fulfilment in human
society was keenly awaited in New Testament times.
Teaching and imagery relating to the Kingdom abound in the
Gospels of Matthew, Mark, Luke and — less obviously — in
St John's Gospel and the New Testament Epistles. However
the theme does appear again in the Book of Revelation. There
the Kingdom of God is contrasted with the kingdoms of this
world (as in the dialogue between Jesus and Pilate in St John's
Gospel). The language of Roman hymns to the earthly
Emperor is borrowed and integrated into hymns in praise of
the God who in Christ has conquered the powers of evil and
will vindicate those who call on him in the midst of
persecution and hardship (see Rev. 5.12; 11.15–17). The
visual language of iconography expresses the kingship of
Christ and his sovereignty over the universe; 'Christ Pantocrator', 'The All ruling Christ' comes to be one of the dominant
themes of Orthodox art, representing the divine Lord who is
the Alpha and the Omega, the source and goal of the Church's
life and worship (*see plates 2, 3 and 18(i)*). The implications of
this iconography have led to strange conflicts between
spiritual and secular authorities in the history of Orthodox
nations, and the arguments involved may seem rather distant
from the teaching in the Gospels, but the inter-relationship of
verbal and visual imagery relating to the themes of Kingdom
and kingship needs to be recognized.

   An image that was closely linked in the minds of early
Christians with the theme of Christ the King is the figure of
the Good Shepherd. The range of associations connected with
this figure in the early Church was very wide. The Good
Shepherd not only represented the implications of the parable
of the Lost Sheep, and the discourse on the Good Shepherd in
St John's Gospel; this figure also represented kingship and
divinity. In Jewish and Greek traditions the ruler was the
shepherd of his people, the one who leads and provides
security; in the Old Testament God is the 'true Shepherd' of

his people (Psalm 23; Ezekiel 34) who leads and provides for the people when earthly shepherds fail. In classical art the figure of the shepherd with a lamb on his shoulders was a common theme, and one which was easily adopted by Christians. In the art of the Roman catacombs this figure comes to represent Christ as God bearing the human nature which the divine Logos assumed. Christ is thus the Saviour of humanity, the One who tends his flock, and leads them through death to the goal of everlasting life.

Another important theme can be seen in the first Epistle to the Corinthians, where St Paul takes up the important Old Testament idea of the Wisdom of God and uses it in relation to the death of Christ. Making great play on contrasting notions of human and divine wisdom, Paul stresses that in the wisdom and providence of God man does not come to know God through earthly wisdom; God's wisdom is revealed to man in the figure of Christ Crucified, a figure who is folly in the eyes of the worldly wise, but the embodiment of divine wisdom to the eye of faith. Not only was wisdom important in Jewish thought, but it was a major theme in the philosophy of other parts of the Mediterranean world. The triple strands of Jewish, pagan and Pauline devotion to wisdom merged to create in the early Church a key theme in Christian theology and spirituality, in honour of which many important churches were dedicated, most notably the church of Hagia Sophia in Constantinople. Holy wisdom was seen as the manifestation of the divine presence and energies, ceaselessly seeking to dwell among men. In Christ and his holy Church, holy wisdom is embodied and revealed; it is celebrated in the liturgy, and set forth before the world in word, sacrament and icon. Icons of Christ often show him holding a scroll, a symbol of the secrets of divine wisdom (*see plates 1 and 13*). Even a church building itself is part of this manifestation of holy wisdom in the Orthodox tradition, for the building is a means of entry into the divine realm of holy wisdom by virtue of the mysteries represented there in iconography and celebrated in the liturgy.

Closely linked to the theme of wisdom is the Word of God, the experience of God speaking to his people. The long history of faith in the Word of God is taken a stage further when the Word is made flesh and dwells among us, becoming man and living among us in the person of Jesus Christ. This theme, which has a prominent place in the Gospel of St John, was developed amid great controversy in the early centuries of Christian history as different groups fought to defend or to deny faith in the divinity and humanity of Christ. Icons of the Mother of God are often painted in such a way as to stress the reality of the incarnation, the reality of the Word made flesh, Emmanuel, God with us. The Blessed Virgin is represented as 'Theotokos', the God-bearer; her Son is no mere babe, but the one who with the scroll in his left hand brings the Word of Life; his right hand is raised in blessing, and the halo or nimbus is around his head as a symbol of divinity (*see plate 1*). As we have already seen, the great controversy about icons in the eighth and ninth centuries was bound up with controversy about the Incarnation, and defenders of icons were the defenders of the faith in the Word made flesh as expressed and defended in the great Councils of the Church.

The Church's preaching from the earliest time made use of verbal and visual imagery in its oral and written traditions, and in some parts of the Gospels one can see how these traditions have been shaped by the imagery and traditions of the Old Testament. A particularly good example of this is in St Mark's Gospel, between 4.35 and 6.56. Here we have a series of stories about Jesus told in a way that echoes material from the Psalms of the Old Testament. The consciousness of those who told the stories was steeped in and shaped by the Old Testament traditions; the Old Testament provided the religious imagery and language through which the evangelist proclaims his message. Thus, the double feeding miracles, the healings of the mentally and physically sick, and the mysterious encounters on the Sea of Galilee are narrated with profound echoes of Old Testament writings which proclaim God's power to save, feed, heal, and calm the turbulence that threatens to overwhelm human life. The stories point to Christ not as a past figure of mere historical interest, but as the ever-present Lord who can bring peace to the afflicted, healing to the sick, and provide the Bread of Life for his

pilgrim Church. The verbal imagery that St Mark uses fulfils
just the same function as some of the image signs and symbols
of God's saving power that are to be found in the catacombs a
little later in the Church's history (for example, Noah in the
ark, Daniel among the lions, and Jonah being saved from the
belly of the whale). Both the verbal imagery of the story and
the visual imagery of the earliest known icons set the life of the
Christian and the Church in the light of the power and
purposes of the God who has become God-with-us in Jesus
Christ.

It is also true, however, that the early parts of each of the
four Gospels in the New Testament are concerned to set
Christ's life and ministry in a historical and theological
context. For St Mark the prophecy fulfilled by John the
Baptist paves the way for the ministry of Jesus. For St John a
major theological discourse sets the scene for the events that
reveal the glory of Christ as the Gospel unfolds. For St
Matthew and St Luke the birth stories and the genealogies are
used to stress the link between the work of God in the past,
and the divine initiative that leads to the birth of Christ and
the New Covenant that He inaugurates) equally these early
chapters in Matthew and Luke show that Jesus Christ cannot
be bounded by the normal categories of human life and
understanding. The narrative element in the Nativity stories
easily translates into visual representations, but icons of the
birth of Christ also stress the theological truths that are being
conveyed in the Gospel narratives and through some of the
additional details given in the Apocryphal Gospels. In the
icons of the Nativity (*see plate 9*) the eye leads the mind and
heart to focus on the mystery of the incarnation, and so
through visual imagery to enter into a silent love of the One
whom heaven and earth adore. The function of the icon and
the function of the Nativity stories is very similar; visual and
verbal imagery are being used to convey to the worshipper the
same faith and open the doors to a perception of the revelation
given in Christ.

III

There are in Orthodox iconography three themes which we
shall look at here that illustrate particularly well the close
inter-relationship of verbal and visual imagery in the New
Testament and in the Orthodox theological tradition as it
developed in the early Christian centuries. In each of the three
examples there is a long tradition of theological and spiritual
teaching between the written material of New Testament
times and the formal iconographic schemes that become
normative for the Orthodox Church; many of the details in
these icons derive from liturgical texts as well as the New
Testament Scriptures. But the inter-relationship of the written
word and the painted icon in these three examples illustrates
very clearly the faith of the seventh Ecumenical Council:
'That which the word communicates by sound, the painting
demonstrates silently by representation'.

At the Transfiguration, Jesus takes Peter, James and John
apart to a high mountain. As we have already seen, many
events of major spiritual significance in the Bible are
associated with mountains; Moses and Elijah experience their
vision of God on Mount Sinai and Mount Horeb, and going
apart up a high mountain is virtually synonymous for an
approach to the mystery of God. It is in this mountain top
experience that Jesus is transfigured, the disciples are
overshadowed by the cloud, and Moses and Elijah stand
talking with Jesus; the voice from the cloud affirms the nature
and authority of the Divine Son whose new dispensation will
shortly fulfil the work of the Law and the Prophets. The
symbolic imagery of the Gospel accounts is taken up into the
language of later Christian spirituality, where the cloud
becomes a symbol both of our ignorance and also of our entry
into the mystery of God's presence. In icons of the Transfiguration (*see plate 16*), the glory of Christ is emphasized as he
is shown transfigured by the Divine Light; the disciples are
filled with awe by the vision, and unable to bear the
brightness of the Divine glory. The icons focus our attention
on Christ as the One who fulfils the Law and the Prophets, the
One in whom the Divine Glory shines forth, and the One who

leads us as he led Peter, James and John to behold his glory.

In St John's Gospel, the raising of Lazarus (chapter 11) has a central place. Christ the Life-Giver comes to the tomb of one who is dead, and his Word of power brings forth the dead man. This work of raising the dead becomes the incident which finally sparks off the attack on Christ that leads to his death — and exaltation. The Life-Giver's work of raising the dead to fulness of life is foreshadowed in the raising of Lazarus, but it will only be completed 'on the last day' when he will raise up those whom the Father has given him (John 6.39–40). For St John this event in the ministry of Jesus has become a symbolic focal point for his understanding of the whole work of God in Christ, and later icons of this event focus on the high points of the drama and their wider spiritual significance (*see plate 13*). The removal of the stone from the tomb becomes a symbol of the removal of all that impedes our entry into new life in Christ. Christ's authoritative 'Word of Life' brings Lazarus into new life, and his enlightenment becomes a source of illumination that sheds light upon the whole scene. These icons point not only to that one particular incident in the Gospel, but to Christ's continuing work of renewal, enlightenment and illumination that is being accomplished through the spiritual tradition of his holy Church. Here again is a tradition mediated through visual and verbal imagery.

The Resurrection of Christ is the crucial event in the whole Gospel narrative, and the subject of the principal Christian festival, Easter; it is the point around which the whole of the liturgical cycle revolves, and the basis of our Baptism into life in Christ. However, the Resurrection remains a mystery, an event beyond human comprehension and not witnessed by human observers. But the consequences of the Resurrection can be represented and celebrated. In Orthodox iconography the chief icon connected with the Resurrection is the icon of the Descent into Hell (*see plates 13 and 18(ii)*). In the New Testament this is mentioned in 2 Peter 3.19 and Acts 2.31 but the imagery used in icons and liturgical texts is coloured by material from the second century apocryphal Gospel of Nicodemus; St Paul's theme of Christ as the Second Adam is also a significant element that needs to be remembered.

The icons of the harrowing of Hell bring together many of the key elements involved in the Church's understanding of the Resurrection, and show the event not simply as an isolated historical occurrence, but as one which has significance for the whole of humanity. Christ, the Second Adam whose obedience and sacrifice has brought about the atonement of God and man, is portrayed as the one who releases humanity from the bondage to sin and death; he breaks open the gates of Hell, releases Adam and Eve, and brings them out with him into the light and glory of the Risen Life which is about to be manifested in the Resurrection; along with Adam and Eve are released the souls of all those who have looked forward in hope to the coming of Christ. In these icons the theology of St Peter and St Paul is combined with the imagery from the Gospel of Nicodemus to convey visually something of the cosmic significance of the redeeming work of Christ; Hell, the underworld, the lower levels of creation and consciousness are all penetrated by the light and glory of the victorious Christ.

These three icons — of the Transfiguration, the Raising of Lazarus, and the Descent into Hell — show very clearly the close correspondence between the verbal texts of the Scriptures, their theological interpretation, and the visual representations in iconographic terms. Because the texts of the Scriptures make use of verbal imagery and a language of symbolism, it is a relatively short step to the development of the visual image of iconography in the sacred tradition of the Orthodox Church. Verbal and visual imagery co-exist in our consciousness, and in the language by which the Church articulates the revelation given in Jesus Christ.

Chapter Five

BIBLICAL INTERPRETATION
Allegory and the influence of Alexandrian Christianity

I

We need now to look in much greater detail at the complex area of the development of the interpretation of the Bible in the first Christian centuries, and its implications for Christian iconography. Modern biblical studies have been influenced by a concern for meticulous historical accuracy that is a relatively recent development; and the way modern Western Christians in a post-Reformation tradition actually look at the Bible is in many respects very different from the approach of Christians in earlier centuries. Modern Western Christians have largely lost touch with the allegorical interpretations of Scripture that were enshrined in the art and architecture of the great medieval cathedrals, and that still form part of the theological language of the Eastern Orthodox tradition. It is some consolation that the interpretation of the Bible has rarely been seen as a simple matter, and modern readers are not the first to find problems with the sacred Scriptures of the Christian Church. At the time of Christ there was a variety of approaches to the Old Testament within Judaism; whatever concern there may have been for the literal or historical meaning of the texts was supplemented by a strong desire to interpret the relevance of the text for a contemporary audience. Nor was this phenomenon something confined to Judaism. As early as the sixth century BC there was a nascent Greek allegorical tradition of interpretation, with exegesis of Homeric literature from a theological or philosophical standpoint. Later interpretation often involved the reading back of newer doctrines into the works of honourable ancient writers.

Thus by the time of Christ in both Jewish and Greek culture there was a dynamic tradition that kept alive ancient material because of its value and significance for the present and the future.

In the New Testament, St Paul frequently shows how fresh meanings can be discovered in or projected back into Old Testament material. In 1 Cor.9 Paul interprets the text 'You shall not muzzle an ox when it treads out the grain' (Deuteronomy 25.4) in terms of the Church's responsibility to provide sustenance for the apostolic ministry. In 1 Cor. 10.4 he uses the image of the rock struck by Moses to provide water in the wilderness (Exodus 17.6; Numbers 20.11) as a symbol of the presence of Christ with the people of the Old Covenant, and a foreshadowing of the Christian rite of Baptism. In Galatians 4.21ff Paul develops a complex allegory involving the two children of Abraham born to Hagar and Sarah; he takes the two women as symbolizing the Old Covenant at Mount Sinai and the New Covenant in Christ, and their children as the people of the Law and the people of the Promise — Judaism and the Church. Thus within St Paul's writing there is already a wide range of styles of interpretation, and this variety increases as time goes by, stimulated to a great extent by the meeting of Jewish, Greek and Christian traditions in the second and third centuries in Alexandria — one of the leading cities of the Roman Empire.

It will help us to gain a richer understanding of the relationship between theology, spirituality and icon painting if we look in some detail at a few of the main streams of thought that were current in Alexandria in these early centuries of the Christian era.

One of the great Alexandrian thinkers, Philo the Jew (c.20 BC–AD 50), stated clearly both the problems relating to scriptural interpretation and the ways they could be solved. Some parts of Scripture he sees as of little literal significance:

'Now Samuel was probably an actual man; but he has been taken by us not as a vital complex of body and soul, but as a mind that rejoices solely in the service and worship of God.'[1]

But even for Philo some allegorizing can go too far:

> 'There are some who taking the laws in their literal sense as symbols of intelligible realities, are over precise in their investigation of the symbol, while frivolously neglecting the letter. Such people . . . ought to have cultivated a more precise investigation of things invisible and an unexceptional stewardship of things viable.'[2]

Philo commends those Jewish contemplatives who . . .

> 'read the Holy Scriptures and apply themselves to their ancestral philosophy by means of allegory, since they believe that the words of the literal text are symbols of a hidden nature, revealed through its underlying meaning.'[3]

> 'The interpretations of the Holy Scriptures are made in accordance with the deeper meanings conveyed in allegory. For the whole of the Law seems to these people to resemble a living being with the literal commandments for its body, and for its soul the invisible meaning stored away in its words. It is in the latter that the rational soul begins especially to contemplate the things akin to itself and, beholding the extraordinary beauties of the concepts through the polished glass of the words, unfolds and reveals the symbols, and brings forth the thoughts bared into the light for those who are able by a slight jog to their memory to view the invisible through the visible.'[4]

In the thought of another of the great Alexandrians, Origen, (c.185–c.254), there is a development of the image of the Scriptures as a living being with body, soul and spirit:

> 'A person ought to describe threefold in his soul the meaning of divine letters . . . so that the simple may be edified by, so to speak, the body of the Scriptures; for that is what we call the ordinary and narrative meaning. But if any have begun to make some progress and can contemplate something more fully, they should be edified by the soul of Scripture. And those who are perfect . . . should be edified by that spiritual Law which has a shadow of the good things to come, edified as by the spirit of Scripture. Thus, just as a human being is said to be made up of body, soul and spirit, so also is sacred Scripture, which has been granted by God's gracious dispensation for man's salvation.'[5]

Origen is quite specific about his view of the intentions of the Holy Spirit in connection with the hidden meaning of the Scriptures:

> 'His [the Holy Spirit's] aim is to envelop and hide secret mysteries in ordinary words under the pretext of a narrative of some kind and of an account of visible things.'[6]

> 'The aim of the Holy spirit, who thought it right to give us the divine Scriptures, is not that we might be able to be edified by the letter alone or in all cases, since we often discover that the letter is impossible or insufficient in itself because by it sometimes not only irrationalities but even impossibilities are described. But the aim of the Holy Spirit is that we should understand that there have been woven into the visible narrative truths that, if pondered and understood inwardly, bring forth a law useful to men and worthy of God.'[7]

> 'And let us think of the Holy Spirit's words not as something that shines as a speech fashioned by frail human eloquence, but, as it is written, "All the king's glory is within" and the treasure of divine meanings is confined, shut up within the frail vessel of the common letter.'[8]

Origen goes on to state that the devout approach to Scripture requires a recognition that it is complex material; a crass literalism will not get very far; some people are in error, because

> 'they understand the Scripture not according to the spiritual meaning but according to the sound of the letter.'[9]

And even the approach to the Gospels, which many expect to be void of complexities, requires the right spiritual approach:

> 'What shall we say when we come to the Gospels? Does not an inner meaning, the Lord's meaning, also lie hidden there that is revealed only by that grace he received who said, "But we have the mind of Christ . . . that we might understand the gifts bestowed upon us by God. And we impart this in words not taught by human wisdom but taught by the Spirit."?'[10]

For Origen the spiritual approach to the Scriptures is shaped by

> 'that rule and discipline which was delivered by Jesus Christ to the apostles and which they delivered in succession to their followers who teach the heavenly Church.'[11]

In other words, scriptural interpretation is made in the light of the Church's faith and tradition; it is not a purely subjective business.

The allegorical approach to the Scriptures, bounded by the teaching of the Church's Creeds, became an integral part of the mainstream Orthodox tradition of theology and spirituality. The spiritual truths that were revealed in the Scriptures came to be regarded as of greater importance than their factual or historical content; a more hidden and profound meaning was believed to exist behind the external and obvious sense of a text. The inner meaning came to have particular significance for some of the sects on the fringe of the Church's life, and the Apocryphal or Non-Canonical Gospels belong to this 'fringe' world of spirituality that was closely related to the mainstream of orthodox Christian teaching, but frequently viewed with great suspicion. However, the fact that a distinction exists between obvious and hidden meanings, between external and inner interpretations of the scriptures within the Orthodox traditions does mean that some of the Apocryphal Gospels are accepted as mediating spiritual truth even if their literal and historical sense is rejected.

In some icons the traditions of the Apocryphal Gospels have to be recognized if one is to understand some of the details of the iconography and their significance; this is particularly true in connection with details of the early life of the Blessed Virgin Mary. For examples of the influence of the Apocryphal Gospels on iconography, see commentary on plates 9, 12 and 15.

II

We must now look at some of the ways Christian faith and spirituality were articulated in the formative early centuries of the Church's life. In doing this we are coming into contact with some strands of the Christian tradition that lie behind the later and more developed theology of the Orthodox Church.

In the development of Christian thinking in the first four hundred years of the Church's history, two great cities of the Roman Empire played a crucial part. At Antioch in Syria, where there had been a vigorous Christian community from the days of the Acts of the Apostles, a theological tradition developed which had a strong sense of the importance of history and the earthly life of Jesus. Biblical exegesis in the Antiochene tradition emphasized the literal meaning intended by the biblical writers; it stressed the humanity of Jesus, and saw the Trinitarian aspect of Christian theology in 'functional' terms; for these theologians the historical working out of the divine plan of salvation involved different modes of operation by the one God who was worshipped as Father, Son and Holy Spirit. In the Antiochene tradition, the heresies which came to be most prevalent were those which under-emphasized the divinity of Christ and the essentially Trinitarian nature of the Godhead.

At Alexandria however, the climate of thought and spirituality was rather different. Here the background of Egyptian religion and the long tradition of Platonic teaching created an atmosphere in which there was a profound sense of the reality and importance of the spiritual world; spiritual reality was more significant than the physical and historical aspects of human life, these latter being seen as mere shadows or pale reflections of reality. At Alexandria the tradition of biblical exegesis was one that looked for hidden meanings in the Scriptures, and found more varied levels of intepretation than the Antiochenes; Christ's human life was primarily important as a vehicle of divine revelation in which the essential nature of the Godhead was made known. The heresies that were most prevalent in the Alexandrian tradition were those which played down the real humanity of Jesus, and whose Trinitarian theology at times came perilously close to tri-theism. The Alexandrian tradition of Christianity had a profound influence on the Church's life and teaching, especially as it is enshrined in the great Creeds of the Church and in Orthodox spirituality.

At the beginning of the Christian era there was already a close inter-relationship between Jewish and Greek thought; these two religious and philosophical traditions were not in separate watertight compartments, as some Christian writers often imply. Jews were dispersed throughout the Graeco-Roman world, and the extensive use of cultural traditions were transmitted throughout the civilized world. Many Jews, it is true, objected to the defilement of their faith and practice by gentile intrusions, but equally there were many who looked more sympathetically at the best that could be found in other cultures. Among these latter Jewish thinkers the most famous and most influential was Philo of Alexandria. He belonged to a prosperous and cultured Jewish priestly family in Alexandria, and, as we have already seen, he was a fertile thinker and writer; his profound sense of the importance of the spiritual and the reality of the inner life meant that he was able to integrate into his thinking both Jewish and gentile religious traditions, and his thought is of great importance to the study of early Christianity in Alexandria. For Philo the Logos (literally 'Word', but also 'principle of expression') was the intermediary between the deity and the world, being both the agent of creation and also the agent of revelation to man. Revelation through the Logos was present in Greek philosophy and in the tradition and writings of the Jews, and in responding to the Logos man found his true spiritual fulfilment. For Philo the Jewish Scriptures were seen as allegories, pointing to spiritual truths beyond the level of merely literal interpretation, and therefore of profound and lasting significance for the soul of man. Thus, for Philo Moses becomes a symbol of one who is in touch with the Logos, and his life becomes a focal point for thought and teaching about the spiritual life; similarly Abraham, Isaac and Jacob represent different types of soul in pursuit of the life of virtue.

Some early Christian teachers feared the influence of pagan philosophy on the faithful. For Tertullian of Carthage (c.160–c.220), Christian belief involved the rejection of philosophy and speculation:

> 'After one has believed there is but one thing more to be
> believed, namely that there is nothing more to be believed.'[12]

In sharp contrast, Clement of Alexandria (c.150–c.215) saw
the need to take seriously the philosophical thought of the
cultured classes, and he gave a much more positive verdict on
the role of Greek philosophy:

> 'Even if Greek philosophy does not comprehend the truth in its
> entirety and, in addition, lacks the strength to fulfil the Lord's
> command, yet at least it prepares the way for the teaching
> which is royal in the highest sense of the word, by making a
> man self-controlled, by moulding his character, and by making
> him ready to receive the truth.
>
>   Greek philosophy, as it were, provides for the soul the
> preliminary cleansing and training required for the reception
> of faith, on which foundation the truth builds up the edifice of
> knowledge.'[13]

To Clement, philosophy was of a divine origin; it fulfilled the
same role of 'paidogogos' (tutor) as Law did in the teaching of
St Paul (cf Galatians 3.24); it was a preparation for Christ and
the truth which he brought to the world.

Clement's great work was continued and given a more
securely Christian basis by Origen, a brilliant pupil of
Clement, and a considerable biblical and speculative theologian; he took over the leadership of the catechetical school in
Alexandria, and in spite of early suspicions about pagan
philosophy he did make it a matter of serious study. Clement
had said,

> 'Anyone who wants to help catechumens, especially if they are
> Greeks, must not shrink from scholarly study.'

Origen, his pupil, fulfilled this duty with the zeal of one who
was committed to making Christianity intelligible to the
thinking people of his day. Although he has never been
accepted as a Doctor of the Church, Origen made a major
contribution to the theological tradition that developed within
the context of Greek philosophy, and included as its great
exemplars St Basil, St Gregory of Nazianzen, St Gregory of

Nyssa and St John Chrysostom, the great heroes of Orthodoxy during the conflicts of the fourth century.

The philosophical tradition that was so important to Clement and Origen laid great stress on the importance of 'knowledge' (Greek: *gnosis*), and saw knowledge as a means whereby the soul of man could make progress. This concern for knowledge also existed among many other religious groups which have been generally classed under the term 'gnostic'. Thus, to many religious and philosophical groups, gnosis was what one needed to make progress up the scale of being; and 'gnosis' was a term that appeared in several Christian writings to express the Church's faith and experience (Romans 15.14; 1 Cor. 1.5; Col. 2.3; 2 Peter 1.5,6.). How did these different forms of *gnosis* relate to one another? Did *gnosis* mean the same thing in each different tradition? These questions lay behind bitter and prolonged divisions within and around the Church. To some groups *gnosis* was part of the spiritual technology one needed in order to reach the higher realms, and an aid in decoding the allegories that shielded the truth in sacred writings from the unenlightened and uninitiated. In a climate of pessimism about the world and the flesh, anything that claimed to show the way to higher things was a great attraction; the Christian Gospel of redemption from sin and evil could easily be seen as a gospel of redemption from an evil world, a way out from the problems and pressures of human life; *gnosis* as a means of salvation could easily become an attractive substitute for obedience to a Saviour who is to be served in the world amid the complexities of the life of his Church. A view of human life that splits off the 'real' soul from the 'illusory' flesh can lead to extreme developments in two opposite directions — great asceticism and holiness, or permissive indulgence in the flesh. Either development can involve the betrayal of the doctrines of Creation and Incarnation. It was these doctrines that Christian opponents of gnosticism fought to uphold: the world as creation, not illusion, and the world as the scene of the divine presence and activity in Jesus Christ and his Church.

Christian theologians claimed to be teaching a true and Christian gnosis, and they made full use of the terminology and imagery in current use. The concept of a scale or hierarchy of being was common in neo-platonic thought, and especially significant in the teaching of the philosopher-mystic Plotinus (c.205–270); in his scheme, at the summit of the hierarchy is the self-sufficient One; beneath the One is the world of Ideas (nous) and then the World Soul (psyche) which mediates between the intelligible and the material worlds, creating the latter and ordering its course; the highest capacity of the human soul is contemplation, achieved through ascetical purification, recollection, and the rejection of the world of the senses. This teaching had much in common with the developing Christian spiritual tradition, but also many major differences; it emphasized the achievement of salvation in contemplation by human effort, in contrast to the Church's stress on the saving work of Christ and grace given through the sacraments, and it held a very different view of creation from that generally accepted within the Church. Yet much of this terminology of neo-platonism was the language that came to be used to articulate the Christian tradition of spirituality.

As early as the teaching of Clement of Alexandria (c.150–c.215), the Christian life was seen as a ladder of ascent whereby the soul progresses from faith to knowledge, love and union with God; the true Christian gnostic grows in sanctification by moral purification, and leaves behind the 'distractions of matter' in his ascent to the heavenly goal. This ladder theme reaches its fullest development in the early seventh century in the work of St John Climacus, and through him passes into the mainstream tradition of spirituality that was the formative background for the icon painters.

III

In studying icons and in using them for devotional purposes we come into contact with a tradition of theology and spirituality that is very different from that familiar to most Western Christians. The icons are not simply illustrations of biblical themes or stories; rather, they are an embodiment of a long tradition of meditation on these themes and incidents, and their significance for man's soul. Just as the theologians who developed the allegorical interpretation of the Scriptures saw in the written text many different levels of truth which they had to interpret and convey, so we who approach icons must be aware of the variety of levels of truth and significance that have been brought together in any one iconographic theme or individual icon. (See also commentary on plates 4, 13 and 15).

Origen said that the aim of the Holy Spirit in the formation of the Scriptures 'is that we should understand that there have been woven into the visible narrative truths that, if pondered and understood inwardly, bring forth a law useful to man and worthy of God'. This comment could equally apply to the work of the Spirit in the creation of icons. In order to receive the fulness of the riches of the Scriptures we have to be prepared for a variety of levels of interpretation; similarly, to receive the riches conveyed through any one icon, we need to be aware of the range of scriptural interpretation that forms part of the theological and religious background of the icon painters. And in the formation of this background, the Alexandrian thinkers we have looked at are highly significant.

Chapter Six

THE SPIRITUALITY OF
THE ICON PAINTERS

I

So far in this book we have considered the origins and development of the Orthodox tradition of icon painting; we looked at the legends which enshrine theological convictions about the importance of icons in the mediating of divine revelation, and the way that early Christian art developed from the simple image-signs of the third century to the fuller iconographic schemes that have become integrated into the worship and consciousness of Orthodox Christians after the conversion of Constantine, and particularly after the resolution of the iconoclast controversy. We looked at the way much of the material in the New Testament was easily 'translated' into the visual language of the plastic arts that was already in existence in the Graeco-Roman world. We have seen how both verbal and visual imagery are part of the language that the Church has used from New Testament times onwards- and we have seen how one particular city — Alexandria — was a centre where Jewish, Gentile and Christian thinkers shared many common attitudes to the spiritual aspect of life and the interpretation of Scripture, and how these thinkers have contributed to the development of the Orthodox theological and spiritual inheritance.

Before considering in detail the visual language of the icons, and how we can enter more fully into what is being conveyed through the icons, one more major topic must be considered: the spirituality of the icon painters. All religious works of art are in some way related to the spirituality of the artists who create them; but this is particular true of icons and those who paint them. One of the central arguments of this book is that we can only truly understand icons by seeing them as expressions of a particular spirituality — the spirituality of the

Orthodox Church, particularly that of its monastic traditions. It is to this spirituality — this way of seeing and experiencing the relationship between God, man, the Church, and the rest of the created order — that we must now turn our attention.

II

An icon painter obviously has to master the skills of his craft; he needs to know his materials and become familiar with the form and scale required for different subjects, yet these technical matters are to be approached with a spirit of reverence and recollection. Dionysius of Fourna, in his *Painter's Manual* already referred to, tells his pupils that even at the stage of copying the work of others they must 'not carry out this work haphazardly, but with the fear of God and with the veneration due to a sacred task'. They are engaging in a 'heavenly task given by God' as they learn the art of painting the holy icons. But this technical skill that has to be mastered is only a part of what is required, for the true iconographer is engaged in a work of spiritual expression; he is not merely repeating a form, but externalizing a spiritual reality that is part of the Orthodox tradition, and should have become a part of himself. The true iconographer has to master the 'science of sciences and art of arts'; he has to be adept in the art and science of prayer of the heart, to be engaged in the work of pure prayer so that his iconography may stem from both the holy tradition and his own experience of the work of grace restoring him in the image and likeness of God.

Of course, not all icon painters have the same depth of spiritual experience and understanding, just as they may not all have the same artistic ability or competence; but the greatest and the least stand in the one tradition of which they are all the servants. However brilliant or pedestrian they and their work may be, the intention is the same: to externalize the sacred tradition and to enable the beholder to enter into the unseen world of the Spirit which transcends and yet inter-penetrates the world of matter and the flesh. The icon painters are not 'illustrators' in the sense that we in the West might speak of illustrations in religious paintings, books or Bibles;

their work is of a different category altogether. Just as the spoken or written word can convey the Church's tradition and deepen the life of faith, so iconography is another means of conveying or externalizing the sacred tradition; and just as spiritual integrity and experience is expected of those who write or preach, so it is of those who undertake the painting of the holy icons. For the purpose of an icon is to take us into the world of the Spirit, where we can experience the transforming power of divine grace.

The Sacred Tradition of which the iconographer is the servant comprises three major aspects. The first is the dogmatic tradition of the Church, expressed primarily in the Bible, the Creeds and other statements of the Councils of the Church, and in the texts of the liturgy. The faith of the Church is central to its life and work, and even if the long controversies of centuries past about heresy sometimes make depressing reading, they are evidence of a concern for truth and for the faithful working out from generation to generation of the revelation given in Christ Jesus. The icon painter as an Orthodox Christian is a servant of the Tradition of that Church, whose art and craft is to bring the mysteries of the faith before the eyes of the faithful for their devout contemplation. Thus, for example, Christ is always depicted in a way that shows him not as an ordinary man, but as the Incarnate One who is the author of our salvation, the Word made flesh (*see plate 9*). Similarly, icons of the Virgin and Child always show Mary as Theotokos, the God-bearer (*see plate 1*).

Second, icon painters are servants of a liturgical tradition. Their work is intimately bound up with the Church's worship — creating some of the most important external elements that form part of the celebration of the liturgy. In some icons the correspondence between the visual representation and the words of the liturgical texts is very clear (see commentary on plates 9 and 10). In many churches the apse contains frescoes or mosaics depicting the celebration of the liturgy, and the Communion of the Apostles, providing a powerful visual link between the heavenly and earthly parts of the Church united in the action of the liturgy. Liturgical poetry also forms the basis for certain iconographic sequences; for example, the twenty-four verses of the Acathist hymn in honour of the Mother of God are often illustrated in frescoes. Wood panel icons, frescoes and mosaics have a liturgical and devotional setting and purpose, and this is true whether they are in churches, homes, or other places.

Third, the great iconographers are servants of a sacred tradition of prayer that lies at the heart of the life of the Orthodox Churches. It is this tradition of spirituality that finds expression in the amazing sense of inner stillness, attentiveness and recollection that is conveyed in many icons (*see plates 5–8*); in responding to these elements in iconography we are, as it were, touching the hem of the garment of a great tradition, and being brought into contact with a tradition of Christian spirituality that has deep roots in the Church's history and has borne fruit in many sanctified and transformed lives. And it is this aspect of the spirituality of icons that we must now look at in greater detail.

III

If we are to understand the Orthodox tradition of prayer we must begin with the nature of our fallen humanity. In the fallen world the image of God in man has become tarnished and man has become enslaved to the passions, to those elements in the spiritual world and the human personality which enslave man and deprive him of his true freedom and dignity. In slavery to the passions, man is turned away from the good and the beautiful and does not make progress in acquiring the likeness of God. Commenting on the terms 'image' and 'likeness' of God, St John of Damascus wrote:

> 'The expression "according to the image" indicates rationality and freedom, while the expression "according to the likeness" indicates assimilation to God through virtue.'[1]

While the image of God in man has not been totally defaced, it is certainly in need of the restoration accomplished by Christ if our vocation to share in the Divine likeness is to be fulfilled; and part of our spiritual work involves the recognizing and dealing with those forces which hold us back from our true vocation, forces which keep us fragmented and distracted, with our God-given energies dissipated in self-indulgence. In *The Life of Moses* St Gregory of Nyssa (c.335–395) speaks of the Egyptian army in pursuit of the children of Israel as an image of the passions which enslave the soul of man:

> 'For who does not know that the Egyptian army — those horses, chariots and their drivers, archers, slingers, heavily armed soldiers, and the rest of the crowd in the enemies' line of battle — are the various passions of the soul by which man is enslaved? For the undisciplined intellectual drives and the sensual impulses to pleasure, sorrow, and covetousness are indistinguishable from the aforementioned army. Reviling is a stone straight from the sling and the spirited impulse is the quivering spear point. The passion for pleasure is to be seen in the horses who themselves with irresistible drive pull the chariot.'[2]
>
> 'For uncontrolled passion is a fierce and raging master to the servile reasoning, tormenting it with pleasures as though they were scourges. Covetousness is another such master who provides no relief to the bondsman . . . And all the other things which are performed by evil are so many tyrants and masters.'[3]

Over against this fallen human nature we can behold the perfect humanity of Christ and the perfected humanity of the Saints. Christ is the Second Adam (1 Cor. 15), the New Man in whom we can find our hope and fulfilment, and in whom we can become what God intends us to be. In Christ we come to share in the image and likeness of God, and experience that work of deification which is the goal of the Spirit's work in us. The Saints represented in Orthodox Churches are there as examples to inspire us, our brothers and sisters in the Communion of Saints; they are the ones who have conquered the passions and in whom the transforming work of grace is fully evident. The inner stillness, recollection and love depicted in the icons of the Saints is set forth as an encouraging example for those still treading the earthly pilgrimage and 'looking to Jesus, the pioneer and perfector of our faith' (Hebrews 12.2). The Saints direct our attention away from themselves to the source of their victory and new life, Christ the New Man in whom we find our true fulfilment.

'It was for the new man that human nature was created at the beginning, and for him mind and desire were prepared. Our reason we have received in order that we may know Christ, our desire in order that we may hasten to Him. We have memory in order that we may carry Him in us . . . He is the resting place of human desires; He is the food of our thoughts; to love anything besides Him or to meditate on it is a manifest aberration from duty and a turning aside from the first principles of our nature.'[4]

(*The Life in Christ*, by Nicholas Cabasilas (born c.1322))

The route from the world of fallen humanity to the perfection of Christ and the Saints is provided within the life of the Church. How this route is delineated in Orthodox teaching can be divided into two paths of sanctification. The first is the path of ordinary church life, with the assimilation of the faith and grace through teaching, the sacraments, prayer and the intention to lead a virtuous and godly life; the second path is a more demanding one within the life of the Church, the hard path through the narrow gate that leads to a fuller possession of the Kingdom of God by means of continuous prayer and recollection. This second path includes the fundamentals of the Christian life that are involved in the first path, but also involves a specific vocation to follow Christ in a life of renunciation of the world; it is essentially, but not exclusively, a monastic path.

As an example of teaching about the first path, *The Life in Christ* by Nicholas Cabasilas deserves to be quoted more fully. This was written as a spiritual guide for Christians living in the world, and possibly, like Nicholas himself, involved in the civic and political affairs of the day. He takes as the framework for his teaching the sacraments of Baptism, Chrismation and the Eucharist; these holy mysteries form a structure to the Christian life which is then developed and enriched through prayer and meditation. In the liturgy the Church celebrates the glory that has been revealed in Christ and the Saints, and which in the Last Day will be revealed in all its fulness. Nicholas is keen to stress the reality of the life in

Christ now, as a gift experienced by the faithful already, yet still awaiting perfection.

> 'The life in Christ originates in this life and arises from it. It is perfected however in the life to come, when we shall have reached the last day . . . Now it is possible for the Son of God to make his friends to share in His Mysteries [i.e. Sacraments] in preparation for that day, and for them to learn from Him what he has heard from the Father. But they must come as His friends who "have ears to hear". Then [i.e. the last day] it is impossible to begin the friendship and to open the ear . . . It is this life that is the workshop for all these things.'[5]

Nicholas stresses the generosity of Christ, and his ever-present help, attracting us and leading us to himself:

> 'There is nothing of which the saints are in need which He is not Himself. He gives them birth, growth and nourishment; He is life and breath. By means of Himself He forms an eye for them and, in addition, gives them light and enables them to see Himself. He is the one who feeds and is Himself the Food; it is He who provides the Bread of Life and who is Himself what He provides . . . Indeed He is the one who enables us to walk; He Himself is the way, and in addition he is the lodging on the way and its destination. We are members, He is the head. When we must struggle, He struggles on our side . . . He turns our mind to Himself from every side and does not permit it to occupy itself with anything else nor to be seized by love of anything else . . . By a wondrous compulsion and gracious governance He draws us to Himself alone and unites us to Himself only.'[6]

He stresses the gift of God's grace and the new life we receive; our part in the work of sanctification is to co-operate with the grace that has been given:

> 'There is an element which derives from God, and another which derives from our own zeal. The one is entirely His work, the other involves striving on our part. However, the latter is our contribution only to the extent that we submit to His grace and do not surrender the treasure nor extinguish the torch that has been lighted.'[7]

For Nicholas the beginning and development of this new life is accomplished through the Sacraments:

> 'Baptism confers being and, in short, existence according to Christ. It receives us when we are dead and corrupted and first leads us to life. The anointing with chrism perfects him who has received new birth by infusing into him the energy that befits such a life. The Holy Eucharist preserves and continues this life and health, since the Bread of Life enables us to preserve that which has been acquired and to continue in life. It is therefore by this Bread that we live and by the chrism that we are moved, once we have received being from the baptismal washing.
>
> In this way we live in God. We remove our life from this visible world to that world which is not seen by exchanging not the place but the very life itself and the mode. It was not ourselves who were moved towards God, nor did we ascend to Him; but it was He who came and descended to us . . . He it was who came to the earth and retrieved His own image, and He came to the place where the sheep were straying . . . He did not remove us from here, but He made us heavenly while yet remaining on earth and imparted to us the heavenly life without leading us up to heaven, but by bending heaven to us and bringing it down.'[8]

In considering this first path of sanctification it is important to remember the full range of spiritual activity and moral development which is assumed to be integrated into the ordinary Christian life. It is not a magical sacramentalism, but the liturgical cycle and the sacraments being used as focal points of Divine activity and of Christian life and worship. Growth in penitence and charity, concern for the duties of society and the nurture of others in the faith are all part of this ordinary path of sanctification that is intended to be the route from the fallen world to the fulness of divine grace in the heavenly kingdom for most Orthodox Christians. Already, the life of the world to come is open to us; that is the central message of hope proclaimed and lived by the Church, and the starting point for individual progress in sanctification.

The second path of sanctification — the more essentially monastic path referred to earlier — is both demanding and

dangerous; hence it has generally been regarded as a special
vocation and one not to be undertaken without appropriate
guidance and support. St Anthony of Egypt (c.251–c.356),
known as the Father of Christian monasticism, felt called as a
young man to give away his possessions, leave all, and follow
Christ in a life of prayer and simplicity away from the
mainstream of secular and religious activity. About the year
AD285 his call took him further into the desert, into solitude,
and into a daunting conflict with the 'demons'. His story is
told by St Athanasius with the 'demonology' taken in a very
literal sense; but even if we may find that sort of terminology
hard to work with today, the reality of Anthony's conflicts,
and the reality of the demonic powers ranged against him are
forces to be reckoned with. Anthony progressed from conventional Christian living in the world to a more demanding life
of prayer and solitude; he was then brought to the stage where
the 'pit of iniquity' was opened up and he was faced with the
multiform reality of evil, and the range of drives, memories
and energies that can possess and destroy the soul of man.
Through long years of prayer and vigilance Anthony emerged
as one who had conquered the demons through the power of
ceaseless prayer and the Name of Jesus Christ; he emerged as
one in whom others could see an authentic wholeness and
sanctity that bore the hallmarks of the life of the world to
come. Anthony came from his conflict in the desert as one in
whom the love of Christ had purged away the roots of evil,
and in whom could be seen a stillness, compassion and
wisdom that had a great power of attraction for others. Many
sought his company and advice, and his life prepared the way
for the whole religious movement of the first monasticism,
whose practical and spiritual wisdom has come down to us in
the 'Sayings of the Desert Fathers'.

The essence of this movement was the rejection of
conventional religious observance in the search for the heroic
quality of sanctity: this was exemplified in Anthony's life. As
we have already seen, after the first two centuries of Christian
history in which martyrdom had been the highest form of
Christian witness, there came an era in which the monastic
life was seen as an equivalent to martyrdom: a laying down of

one's life and a rejection of all worldly values in the service of Christ alone. In the lives of the desert fathers it was not the power of the Roman Empire that had to be endured for the sake of the faith, as in the days of the martyrs; it was the power of evil itself that had to be faced in prayer and in the Name of Jesus. The demons had to be recognized and deprived of their power over the soul of man; evil had to be unmasked in this spiritual warfare, to be revealed, and conquered by the power of Christ. In this battle, unceasing prayer is the chief weapon whereby evil is to be overcome and the goal of our pilgrimage attained. And the place of the battle is in the heart of man. The movement away from the cities to the desert was a movement away from the external distractions of life to the solitude where the real warfare could be waged; in this, the desert fathers were inspired by the example of Christ himself who had been driven into the wilderness by the Spirit after his Baptism, in order to be with the wild beasts and be tempted by the devil.

In this second path of sanctification the material at hand to help with the journey and the inner warfare is found in the writings of those who have trodden the same path, and in the spiritual guidance available from those who are recognized as living masters of what has been called the 'science of science and art of arts'. There have been over the Christian centuries many great guides and spiritual fathers to whom people could turn for direction and help. In Russia in the last century, for example, there were many such startzi (plural of staretz, elder or spiritual guide), some of whom, such as St Seraphim of Sarov (1759–1833), Staretz Amvrosy (1812–91) and Staretz Silouan of Mount Athos (1866–1938), have become reasonably well known in Western Christian circles.

Apart from such living sources of spiritual wisdom and discernment, there are major texts that give guidance in the journey to sanctification. St John Climacus (c.570–649) wrote the *Ladder of Divine Ascent* for this purpose — to provide guidance for those at St Catharine's Monastery on Mount Sinai. Although his book is primarily written for monks, the teaching given is by no means exclusively monastic in its application. Similarly the *Discourses* of St Symeon the New

Theologian (949–1022) are based on teaching he gave to his monks at the monastery of St Mamas in Constantinople in his zeal to open others to the experience of that grace of the Holy Spirit which was so real to him.

Above all others, however, one text stands out in any consideration of the spiritual teaching of the Orthodox Church. In 1782 a collection of writings ranging from the fourth to the fifteenth centuries was published under the title of *The Philokalia* (Greek for 'love of the beautiful'). In this collection St Nicodemus of the Holy Mountain (1749–1809) and St Makarios of Corinth (1731–1805) brought together much of the teaching of the Orthodox monastic tradition that had for many generations given guidance to those on the path where 'the intellect is purified, illumined and made perfect'. The texts of *The Philokalia* are not concerned with intellectual development in the Western sense; they have little to do with our discursive, reasoning faculty. In these texts, 'intellect' means that capacity of the soul of man whereby we may come to know God and gain a higher perception of the truth; similarly in this tradition, 'the heart' means the spiritual centre of man's being, and 'prayer of the heart' means prayer of the whole being. The way that is enshrined in *The Philokalia* is a way of inner work, wherein man is purified, illumined, and brought to an awakened consciousness of himself and of God that will lead to his spiritual fulfilment and sanctification; it is no easy path to tread, but one which will involve conflict with the vices and the distorted powers of the soul before the final victory can be won.

The path as set forth by St John Climacus involves thirty steps on the ladder of divine ascent, corresponding to the thirty years of our Lord's life at the time of his Baptism. The first steps involve renunciation of the worldly life and detachment from the cares of this world in order to set out on the monastic vocation. Obedience, penitence, remembrance of death, and mourning are the fundamental virtues that have to be acquired before the struggle with the passions can be undertaken. John devotes much attention to this struggle, writing not only of the vices, but also of their opposing virtues. Then comes attention to the higher virtues of simplicity, humility and discernment. In all this John displays a sober realism and does not want his readers to be led astray by such ephemeral distractions as dreams, visions and ecstasies. Then comes the goal of the journey: union with God in stillness, prayer, dispassion, faith, hope and love. It should perhaps be mentioned that monastic illustrations of the ladder theme show many monks falling off, or being pulled off the ladder by demons; this path to the perfection of Divine Love is a daunting one, and not all reach the goal. Dionysius of Fourna describes the iconography of this theme:

'A monastery: outside its gates is a crowd of monks, both young and old, and before them is a great ladder reaching up to heaven. Monks are on it, some climbing, others just beginning to mount; above them winged angels make as if to help them. At the top is Christ in heaven, and before him is the topmost rung of the ladder, from which an old and venerable monk reaches out his hands to him and looks at him. Christ with one hand receives him gladly and with the other places on his head a crown of various flowers, saying to him: "Come unto me all ye that travail and are heavy laden, and I will give you rest." Below the ladder is a crowd of winged demons, clutching at the tunics of the monks; some of them drag at the monks but are unable to pull them down, while others pull them a little way from the ladder, (some of the monks seizing the ladder with one hand or both hands); others are pulled completely away, and the demons hold them round the waist with their faces downwards. Beneath them the all-devouring Hell is shown as a great and fearful dragon, with a monk between his jaws of whom only the feet are visible.'[9]

The following extracts give some indication of the goal St John Climacus has in mind for those who follow this path, and also some idea of his warmth and humour.

On stillness:

'The cat keeps hold of the mouse. The thought of the hesychast [one who practises the prayer of stillness] keeps hold of his spiritual mouse. Do not mock the analogy. Indeed, if you do so, it shows you still do not understand the meaning of stillness.'[10]

'He who has achieved stillness has arrived at the very centre of the mysteries, but he would never have reached these depths if he had not first seen and heard the sound of the waves and of the evil spirits, if he had not even been splashed by those waters.'[11]

'Let the remembrance of Jesus be present with your every breath. Then indeed you will appreciate the value of stillness.'[12]

On prayer:

'Rise from love of the world and love of pleasure. Put care aside, strip your mind, refuse your body. Prayer, after all, is a turning away from the world, visible and invisible. What have I in Heaven? Nothing. What have I longed for on earth besides You? Nothing, except to cling always to You in undistracted prayer. Wealth pleases some, glory others, possessions others, but what I want is to cling to God and to put the hopes of my dispassion in Him.[13]

'If prayer is a matter of concern to you, then show yourself to be merciful.'[14]

'Always be brave, and God will teach you your prayer.'[15]

'You cannot discover from the teaching of others the beauty of prayer. Prayer has its own special teacher in God, who "teaches man knowledge".'[16]

On dispassion:

'So here we are, stuck in the deepest pit of ignorance, in the dark passions of the body, in death's shadow, and still we have the temerity to hold forth on the subject of heaven on earth!

Stars adorn the skies and dispassion has the virtues to make it beautiful. By dispassion I mean a heaven of the mind within the heart, which regards the artifice of demons as a contemptible joke. A man is truly dispassionate . . . when he has cleansed his flesh of all corruption; when he has lifted his mind above everything created, and has made it master of all the senses; when he keeps his soul continually in the presence of the Lord.'[17]

'The dispassionate man no longer lives himself, but it is Christ who lives in him'.[18]

'Blessed dispassion raises the poor mind from earth to heaven, raises the beggar from the dunghill of passion. And love, all praise to it, makes him sit with princes, that is with the holy angels, and with the princes of God's people.'[19]

On love:

> 'If sight of the one we love clearly makes us change completely, so that we turn cheerful, glad and carefree, what will the face of the Lord not do as He comes to dwell, invisible, in a pure soul?'[20]

> [Love] is an abyss of illumination, a fountain of fire, bubbling up to inflame the thirsty soul. It is the condition of angels, and the progress of eternity.'[21]

The Philokalia contains works that are both earlier and later than the time of St John Climacus, but they are all part of the same spiritual tradition. The authors whose works are brought together in *The Philokalia* are often called the 'Wakeful Fathers' because of their stress on wakefulness and alertness in the spiritual life. Distraction is to be avoided, so that the intellect can be free to turn to God as the passions are conquered and the powers of the soul fulfil their proper function. Prayer of the heart occupies a prominent place in the teaching of *The Philokalia*, often in the form of the 'Jesus Prayer': 'Lord Jesus Christ, Son of God, have mercy on me', or 'Lord Jesus Christ, Son of God, have mercy on me a sinner'. This prayer repeated continuously in the heart, and often linked with the breathing, is a way of honouring the injunction given by St Paul that we should pray without ceasing (1 Thess. 5.17). By this prayer the whole of one's being is gathered up before God, in the faith that He who came to share our humanity did so in order that we might experience his loving-kindness and enter into full communion with him. The prayer is both simple and profound: simple, as a short phrase which can become an anchor for the mind and the heart; profound, as a phrase that sums up much of the dogmatic teaching of the Church on which our faith and spirituality are to be built. It is a way of praying that can drive away distractions and temptation, and lead the heart of man to a warmth and illumination in the presence of God. It is not surprising that this way of praying has found increasing application among those who live 'in the world', and that *The Philokalia* is regarded as a treasure house of wisdom by many who are outside the Orthodox Church and monastic institutions.

The way of praying taught in *The Philokalia* is often described as 'Hesychasm', from the greek word *hesychia*, which conveys the meaning of stillness, tranquility and being concentrated in attentiveness. The hesychast tradition goes back very early in the history of Christian spirituality, at least to the desert fathers and other early teachers, and has been a powerful force in Orthodox monastic life. At various times great revivals of this way of praying have spread through different parts of the Church; one such revival on Mount Athos in the thirteenth and fourteenth centuries spread widely from Greece into Bulgaria, Serbia and Russia. Moreover, there seems to be a very close link between hesychasm in Russian monasticism and the great flowering of Russian iconography in the fourteenth and fifteenth centuries. It has been suggested — as mentioned previously — that the great work of Andrei Rublev and his school is an externalization of the spiritual tradition of hesychasm that was developed in Russia through St Sergius (1314–92) and his disciples.

IV

The following quotations have been selected from *The Philokalia* to give some sense of the style and content of that work, and further illustrate the type of spirituality that lies behind the great tradition of icon painting. The quotations are best read slowly, and then used as a basis for reflection and prayer. Some of the texts given here and some of the icons reproduced in this book can be seen as illuminating one another; the texts and the icons are both externalizations of a great tradition of spiritual experience.

1. The path of true wisdom:

> 'With all your strength pursue the virtue of attentiveness — that guard and watch of the intellect, that perfect stillness of

heart and blessed state of the soul when free from images, which is all too rarely found in man.

This is the path of true spiritual wisdom. In great watchfulness and fervent desire travel along it with the Jesus Prayer, with humility and concentration, keeping the lips of both the senses and the intellect silent, self-controlled in food and drink and in all things of a seductive nature; travel along it with a mind trained in understanding, and with God's help it will teach you things you had not hoped for; it will give you knowledge, enlightenment and instruction of a kind to which your intellect was impervious while you were still walking in the murk of passions and dark deeds, sunk in forgetfulness and in the confusion of chaos.'[22]

'When the heart has acquired stillness it will perceive the heights and depths of knowledge; the ear of the still intellect will be made to hear marvellous things from God.[23]

2. On abandoning the passions:

'When Moses tried to draw near to the burning bush he was forbidden to approach until he had loosed his sandals from his feet. If, then, you wish to behold and commune with Him who is beyond sense-perception and beyond concept, you must free yourself from every impassioned thought.'[24]

'You cannot attain pure prayer while entangled in material things and agitated by constant cares. For prayer means the shedding of thoughts.'[25]

'A man who is tied up cannot run. Nor can the intellect that is a slave to passion perceive the realm of spiritual prayer. For it is dragged about by impassioned thoughts and cannot stay still.'[26]

'Many passions are hidden in the souls; they can be checked only when their causes are revealed.'[27]

'None but Jesus Christ Himself, unifier of what is disunited, can give your heart lasting peace from passions.'[28]

3. Prayer and the memory:

'When you pray, keep close watch on your memory, so that it does not distract you with recollections of your past. But make

yourself aware that you are standing before God. For by
nature the intellect is apt to be carried away by memories
during prayer.

While you are praying, the memory brings before you
fantasies either of past things, or of recent concerns, or of the
face of someone who has irritated you.

The demon is very envious of us when we pray, and uses
every kind of trick to thwart our purpose. Therefore he is
always using our memory to stir up thoughts of various things
and our flesh to arouse the passions, in order to obstruct our
way of ascent to God.'[29]

4. Conflict:

'If you cultivate prayer, be ready for the attacks of demons and
endure them resolutely; for they will come at you like wild
beasts and maltreat your whole body.'[30]

5. Demons:

'The intellect cannot conquer a demonic fantasy by its own
unaided powers, and should never attempt to do so. The
demons are a sly lot: they pretend to be overcome and then trip
us up by filling us with self-esteem. But when we call upon
Jesus Christ, they do not dare to play their tricks with us even
for a second.'[31]

'Their unremitting purpose is to prevent the heart from being
attentive, for they know how greatly such attentiveness
enriches the soul.'[32]

'A person's heart will not be freed from demonic thoughts,
words and actions until it has first purified itself inwardly,
uniting watchfulness with the Jesus Prayer.'[33]

6. Purification of the heart:

'He who wishes to cleanse his heart should keep it continually
aflame through practising the remembrance of the Lord Jesus,
making this his only study and his ceaseless task. Those who
desire to free themselves from their corruption ought to pray
not merely from time to time but at all times; they should give

themselves always to prayer, keeping watch over their intellect even when outside places of prayer. When someone is trying to purify gold, and allows the fire of the furnace to die down even for a moment, the material which he is purifying will harden again. So too, a man who merely practises the remembrance of God from time to time, loses through lack of continuity what he hopes to gain through his prayer. It is a mark of one who truly loves holiness that he continually burns up what is worldly in his heart through practising the remembrance of God, so that little by little evil is consumed in the fire of this remembrance and his soul completely recovers its natural brilliance with still greater glory.'[34]

7. Detachment:

'Detachment is the mark of a perfect soul, whereas it is characteristic of an imperfect soul to be worn down with anxiety about material things.'[35]

'He who dwells continually within his own heart is detached from the attractions of the world, for he lives in the Spirit and cannot know the desires of the flesh.'[36]

'All men are made in God's image; but to be in His likeness is granted only to those who through great love have brought their own freedom into subjection to God. For only when we do not belong to ourselves do we become like Him who through love has reconciled us to Himself. No one achieves this unless he persuades his soul not to be distracted by the false glitter of this life.'[37]

8. Patience and humility:

'Do not lose heart and despair because you have not yet received the gift of prayer. You will receive it later.'[38]

'Cultivate great humility and courage, and you will escape the power of the demons.'[39]

'Light is the property of a star, as simplicity and humility are the property of a holy and God-fearing man. Nothing distinguishes more clearly the disciples of Christ than a humble spirit and a simple way of life.'[40]

'Just as when light is absent, all things are dark and gloomy, so when humility is absent, all our efforts to please God are vain and pointless.'[41]

9. Silence, stillness and spiritual knowledge:

'When the door of the steam bath is continually left open, the heat inside rapidly escapes through it; likewise the soul, in its desire to say many things, dissipates its remembrance of God through the door of speech, even though everything it says may be good ... Timely silence, then is precious, for it is nothing less than the mother of the wisest thoughts.'[42]

'If you wish to engage in spiritual warfare, let that little animal, the spider, always be your example for stillness of heart; otherwise you will not be as still in your intellect as you should be.'[43]

'Spiritual knowledge illuminates man through its inner energy while wisdom does so through being expressed outwardly. Spiritual knowledge comes through prayer, deep stillness and complete detachment, while wisdom comes through humble meditation on Holy Scripture and, above all through grace given by God.'[44]

10. Guarding the heart and the intellect:

'Be attentive to yourself, so that nothing destructive can separate you from the love of God. Guard your heart, and do not grow listless.'[45]

'Stand guard and protect your intellect from thoughts while you pray. Then your intellect will complete its prayer and continue in the tranquility that is natural to it. In this way He who has compassion on the ignorant will come to you, and you will receive the blessed gift of prayer.'[46]

'The guarding of the intellect is a watchtower commanding a view over our whole spiritual life.'[47]

11. Attentiveness and watchfulness:

'Watchfulness is a way embracing every virtue, every commandment, It is the heart's stillness, and when free from mental images, it is the guarding of the intellect.'[48]

'Continuity of attention produces inner stability; inner stability produces a natural intensification of watchfulness; and this intensification gradually and in due measure gives contemplative insight into spiritual warfare. This in turn is succeeded by persistence in the Jesus Prayer and by the state that Jesus confers, in which the intellect, free from all images, enjoys complete quietude.'[49]

'Attentiveness is the heart's stillness, unbroken by any thought. In this stillness the heart breathes and invokes, endlessly and without ceasing, only Jesus Christ who is the Son of God and Himself God.'[50]

'Much water makes up the sea. But extreme watchfulness and the Prayer of Jesus Christ, undistracted by thoughts, are the necessary basis for inner vigilance and unfathomable stillness of soul . . . This watchfulness and this Prayer must be intense, concentrated and unremitting.'[51]

'Be watchful as you travel each day the narrow but joyous and exhilarating road of the mind, keeping your attention humbly in your heart . . . and invoking Jesus Christ.'[52]

'Watchfulness and the Jesus Prayer . . . mutually reinforce each other.'[53]

12. The Jesus Prayer:

'With your breathing combine watchfulness and the name of Jesus, or humility and the unremitting study of death. Both may confer great blessing.'[54]

'Truly blessed is the man whose mind and heart are as closely attached to the Jesus Prayer and to the ceaseless invocaton of His name as air to the body or flame to the wax. The sun rising over the earth creates daylight; and the venerable and holy name of Jesus, shining continually in the mind, gives birth to countless intellections radiant as the sun.'[55]

'He who wishes to cleanse his heart should keep it continually aflame through practising the remembrance of the Lord Jesus, making this his only study and ceaseless task.'[56]

V

The spiritual path delineated in the writings of *The Philokalia* and other similar works was followed mainly in a monastic setting. It is important for Western Christians to know that in the Orthodox Church the monastic vocation has been worked out in three main ways. First, there have been the hermits (the eremetic life), those like St Anthony of Egypt who went off to live a solitary life in the deserts of the Middle East, the forests of Russia, or in any other appropriate situation away from the routine activity of human society. Second, there have been the monasteries with a strong communal life; these have included extremely large communities as well as smaller groups of monks: St Pachomius of Egypt (292 to 346) — a former soldier in the Roman army — was the great pioneer in this field, and his work had great influence in both the Eastern and the Western Church through the way it was developed by both St Basil and St Benedict as they made further strides forward in the organization of monastic communities in both East and West. Third, there is the 'semi-eremetic' life, consisting of loosely grouped settlements and communities, often quite small in number, and very much under the guidance of a spiritual elder who was only occasionally a priest: in fourth-century Egypt, Nitria and Scetis were great centres for this form of monasticism. Sometimes, as in the region of St Catherine's Monastery in the days of St John Climacus, all three forms of the monastic life could be found in the same area; the same is true of the Holy Mountain of Athos in Greece at the present time, where large monasteries, hermit-ages and 'sketes' still exist on the same peninsula that has been set aside for the monastic life since the tenth century.

Throughout the history of the Byzantine Empire the

monastic life was also very important in the major cities, especially Constantinople, the capital and nerve centre of the Empire. Many famous monasteries provided great leaders for the Church and exercised great influence on affairs of state. Here, as elsewhere, there were strong links between monastic houses and developments in the cultural and artistic life of the church. The very best quality work was done in major church building developments; and while iconography may have been influenced by secular artistic developments, it remained a prime concern of church authorities. Different workshops or schools of iconography had their influence within the Byzantine world, but all were working with a sacral view of human society, in which the spiritual realm interpenetrated the secular world. Indeed, the Byzantine Empire was seen as an icon of the Kingdom of God, a sacred society with a spiritual as well as a political authority and purpose. It may be difficult for us to enter into the thinking and assumptions of such a society, but unless we do, we shall never appreciate the way that Orthodox spirituality, art, and political life are so closely interrelated.

As the Orthodox Church spread into Russia from the tenth century onwards, so the monastic life became a central part of Russian life, and the traditions of spirituality looked at in this chapter became an integral part of the Russian Orthodox Church. In 1051 the Monastery of the Caves was founded at Kiev by St Anthony (983 to 1073), and later reorganized by St Theodosius (died 1074). Anthony had spent some time on Mount Athos, while Theodosius was influenced by the Rule of the monastery of Studium at Constantinople. These early saints of Kievan Russia were marked by a profound humility and self-emptying, a concern for the needs of the poor, and by a willingness to sacrifice their lives for the sake of Christ. The links between Kiev and Byzantium meant that ideals of spirituality, art and political organization of Kievan Russia had much in common with those of Byzantium. As trade links to the north were explored by Christian missionaries places like Novgorod and Pskov in their turn became outposts of the same Christian culture, even though local influences shaped particular aspects of their development.

During the period when the Mongols held power over most of Russia (mid-thirteenth to mid-fifteenth centuriies), one of the most important movements in Russian religious history took place, and this too was an extension of the true Orthodox tradition. Sergius of Radonezh (c.1314 to c.1392 *see plate 8*), like St Anthony of Egypt, felt called to withdraw to the solitary life of prayer; he went off ito the forests and founded his hermitage dedicated to the Holy Trinity. After many years in solitude he was joined by others who came to be his disciples. As their staretz he formed this group into a monastic community, and from the Holy Trinity Lavra many other eremetical and monastic foundations were established, taking the Church and its culture far into the northern forests as the monastic life became an instrument for conversion and civilization in these remote areas. St Sergius exemplified the spiritual traditions of Kievan and Byzantine monasticism, and his work was nourished by close links with the spirituality and art of Byzantium. And it was the hesychast tradition of the fourth century desert fathers which was at the heart of the spiritual renewal that took place around St Sergius. This period — 1350 to 1550 — is often referred to as the golden age of Russian spirituality, a period that saw the creation of many of the finest Russian icons, icons which can only be understood as an externalization of the great Orthodox spiritual tradition.

Chapter Seven

THE VISUAL LANGUAGE OF ICONS

As mentioned at an earlier stage in this book, Russia became the main focus of icon painting during the period between, roughly speaking, the fifteenth and nineteenth centuries. But in the seventeenth century, a decline in the great tradition of icon painting in Russia began. This was in great part due to the impact of Western values on Russian society at the time of Peter the Great, and particularly the influence of Western post-Renaissance religious art. The concern with the natural world and the human form that was so important in Western art at that time was in direct conflict with the artistic traditions of the Orthodox Church. In the seventeenth century there were some Russian icon painters like Joseph Vladimirov who ridiculed the ancient traditions of Russian Orthodox art in his ambition to promote the realistic representations that were common in Western religious art. He and others like him shared Peter the Great's zeal for things from the Western world, and accelerated the change away from the sacred artistic tradition. In this drastic change it is obvious that more than art was at stake: the Russian deovtees of Western art had lost touch with the inner life of their own sacred tradition and the purpose that lay behind the painting of icons. The fact that they had such a desire to be 'realistic' in the Western sense in their religious art reveals that they had lost sight of the great Orthodox tradition of icon painting which was essentially a non-naturalistic art. The essence of the Orthodox tradition was to make visible that which could not be perceived by the ordinary senses, and create a way into the realm of transfigured humanity.

As we have seen, the great tradition of iconography was inextricably linked with prayer and that spiritual path set forth in *The Philokalia*; the icons reflected and mediated that stillness and attentiveness, not by the techniques of the

Renaissance artist, but by a visual language that was consistently used through most of the Orthodox world. The Russian decline was matched by a later, but equally serious loss of purpose elsewhere in the Orthodox world. This decline began to be reversed in the latter part of the last century in Russia with the work of the Slavophil movement — a movement that was concerned to re-discover the distinctive traditions of Orthodoxy and escape from the distorting influences of Western theology and art. In this century in Greece there has been a similar reaction against sentimentality in style, and a revival of the great tradition of icon and fresco painting with the work of people like Photios Kontoglou. Much of the wisdom of the old living tradition has inevitably been lost; but the fact that there is renewed interest in the great tradition of icon painting and in the spirituality of *The Philokalia* is a hopeful sign that Orthodox art will recover something of its former power and eloquence.

In approaching icons we are entering a world where a different language is used: the non-verbal language of visual semantics, the symbolic language of form and colour. To people accustomed to naturalistic art the learning of this different language of silence can be a hard task; it is a task where we must look and listen, a task in which silence, stillness and attentiveness are our greatest assets. The comments made in this chapter on this langauge are not intended to 'explain' icons, but to clear away some widely held misconceptions and possibly provide some keys to unlock these doors of perception.

It is perhaps surprising that many people still comment on the 'oddness' of many features within an icon. The face, the gestures, the proportions of the body, or the general surroundings of a scene may cause people to describe icons as being in some way primitive art. Such a reaction normally means that the first lesson has yet to be learnt: icons are not intended to be looked at as naturalistic works of art. We must forget what we normally call the 'natural world'; and we must forget most of the assumptions of Western religious art. Only then can we begin to look at icons on their terms and not ours. We have to learn to become more intuitive, or to accept what we first find intuitively attractive about an icon, and then work on from there; that may give us some powerful clue about the meaning of an icon or its message, and we will then go on to explore the bond that is established between the icon and ourselves. Then in the stillness we shall discover that we are receiving something that speaks in silence to the very centre of our being.

Reference was made in chapter five (p.52) to the neo-platonic view of the world with different levels of being, ranging from evil at the lowest level, up through matter and human life to the world of the spirit and angelic beings, and then above the whole hierarchy, the deity itself. Without necessarily accepting all the details of any particular neo-Platonic scheme, this idea of the scale of being needs to be recognized as a 'hidden agenda' behind many icons. They speak of the movement to the 'higher life'; progress to the 'angelic state'; the progress of the soul from the realm of the passions to a full union with God in dispassion, stillness and deification. In some icons the dark lower levels, or a cave in one corner, may be taken to represent the lowest levels of existence (*see plates 6, 10 and 14*), while at the top a circle or segment of a circle or a hand will represent the Divine Presence (*see plates 6 and 9*). In some icons there may be a ladder forming part of the scene, as in some icons of the Crucifixion; the significance of the ladder may well be linked to the purpose of the spiritual life, to that ladder of divine ascent which can only be climbed by a way of self-negation after the example of Christ who gave himself upon the Cross. In other icons there may be a very strong sense of tension or balance between the higher and lower levels represented in the icon (*see plate 16*); the representation of saints on horseback is frequently a presentation of those who are in control of the passions and in harmony with the God-given energies of the human soul. Again there may be a strong diagonal movement which hints at the scale of being, portraying the spiritual journey or else the incarnational movement of Divine grace from the heavenly realm to the earthly level. The level at which people are placed in relation to one another is often significant; a staretz will always be placed higher than his disciples (*see plate 6*), while in icons of

Christ among the Doctors (Luke 2.46) it is the young Christ who is at a higher level than the Jewish doctors of the Law.

Just as the hesychast tradition urges watchfulness and attentiveness, so many icons convey a sense of stillness and inner recollection (*see plates 5, 6, 7 and 8*). This is partly achieved through the use of certain techniques in design which create a sense of poise, harmony and order. In icons of Christ in Glory the figure of Christ is enclosed within a red diamond shape, within the dark oval mandorla, within a red rectangle, in whose four corners are the symbols of the evangelists receiving rays of light from the Lord in the centre; the red diamond and rectangle make up an octagonal star, and the whole composition is so 'centred' that one cannot help being drawn into the harmony and balance of the icon of him in whom 'all things hold together' (Colossians 1.17, *see plate 2*). Sometimes a strong triangular pattern lies within an icon (*see plates 1 and 18(i)*), a hidden structure around which the whole composition is built up; or it may be that a circle is the unseen unifying structural factor which keeps the various elements united in a harmonious order or balance (*see plates 3, 4 and 15*). Often there can be a profound sense of controlled energy held in creative tension (*see plate 7*), pointing to that inner work of prayer and purification that lies at the heart of the Orthodox tradition. Another technique which is often used in icons of individual saints is axial symmetry; here a very strong central line forms the organizational centre around which the icon is built up (*see plate 8*); it is often used in icons which include border scenes from the life of a saint; the standing figure of the saint has a stability and inner balance that provide the focus around which the various details of the saint's life are assembled.

In much post-Renaissance Western painting, the lines of perspective lead into the distance to converge at some point in infinity, the size of people represented decreasing the further back they are in the picture. In many icons things are quite different, through the use of an inverse perspective; when this technique is used, the lines of perspective are reversed, to converge not at some distant point in the scene, but in front of the icon in the eyes of the beholder; one is left feeling that the beholder is essential to the completion of the icon. The essence of the exercise has been to establish a communion between the event or persons represented in the icon and those who stand before it, to 'make present' to another person what is presented in the icon (*see plate 11*). This technique helps to fix attention on the icon by preventing the eyes wandering beyond the figures represented. Other deliberate distortions of normal perspective are also used, often in conjunction with inverse and normal perspective; this can lead to the recognition that our normal everyday world is also the scene where events of an inner or higher or spiritual world are taking place, a world where our normal values and assumptions are turned upside down. To enter into this world, our minds must be converted, and we must pass through the narrow gate that leads to life (Matthew 7.13–14). Our own perspectives have to be changed as we enter into the realms that the icons open·up for us; communication takes place in the stillness, and the leaving behind of the normal external world leads to the cosmos transfigured in the light of Christ.

The techniques involved in the use of light and colour create a sense that we are looking into a world illuminated not by an external light that casts shadows, but by the light of divine grace that transforms buildings and landscapes (*see plates 6 and 17*), and is particularly manifested in the inner illumination of the saints. In icons of the Transfiguration, the light of the Transfigured Christ illuminates the whole scene (*see plate 16*); similarly in icons of the Raising of Lazarus, it is from the one who has been awakened from the dead that the light shines forth (*see plate 13*), representing the illuminating power of one who has been released from the passions that bind the soul and entered the state of 'blessed dispassion'. In much Christian and neo-platonist philosophy there has been great stress on the role of light as a mediator between the world of matter and spirit; in the work of the great iconographers we can see the qualities of light and colour being used to mediate the world of the Spirit to us, and to take us to the point where man can share in the glory of the transfigured creation.

In some icons a ray of light from the top of the icon

indicates a movement from the heavenly realm to the earth where particular events are taking place. In his *Painter's Manual* Dionysius of Fourna ends his instructions for icons of the Nativity of Christ with this detail: 'Above in the midst of the angels is the star, with a broad ray coming down on to the head of Christ'[1] (*see plate 9*). In icons of the Baptism of Christ a similar device is specified: 'Above is heaven, and out of it the Holy Spirit in a ray of light descends on to the head of Christ'.[2] A similar requirement is given in Dionysius's instructions for icons of the Annunciation to the Mother of God. Not only do these rays of light help focus our attention at a particular point in the icon, they stress the divine origin and purpose behind the incident represented there.

The buildings represented in icons form perhaps the most obvious non-naturalistic elements in an icon (*see plates 4, 11, 12 and 17*); pillars can be placed directly over a hole in a building; windows and doors can be in architecturally impossible positions; and the general structure and design of a building often has more in common with something from the dream state of the unconscious mind than with anything likely to be seen in even the most exotic parts of the Byzantine or Russian worlds. In later icons, things are tidied up and made more logical; pictures of real and realistic buildings begin to be used as the symbolic significance of the buildings is lost. The 'unrealistic' buildings are part of the visual language of the icon painters; they can represent the setting of the event portrayed, but by being non-naturalistic these buildings help to show that the event and its significance are not confined to a precise historical moment of time and space; they belong to the world of the spirit, to a world of human consciousness that is richer and more mysterious than the ordinary everyday world of rational decisions and logical actions. The wider significance of the events portrayed has to be worked out in the soul of those who behold the icon; what the icon represents may have been manifested at a precise point in time and space, but its fuller significance is found in the inner world where the true work of purification, illumination, and union have to be accomplished. Thus the non-realistic buildings used as the setting in an icon can open up to us the awareness that it is our own inner world that is being addressed, and to which our attention is being directed. The illumination given by a specific event or person and set forth in the icon has to be accomplished in our souls also.

Two other details of the 'surroundings' that are common in icons are a tree and — as we have already noted — a mountain peak. The tree is a symbol of the Tree of life (Genesis 2.9; 3.24 and Revelation 22.1–2) and spiritual growth, while the mountain top, as in the Bible, is a symbol of an event of profound spiritual significance. Often these symbols are much distorted, as if to reinforce their symbolic function and their place in the whole visual language of iconography (*see plate 4*).

In the representation of the human form there is a similar range of what people in the Western tradition have come to think of as 'distortions', used in a consistent way to represent the dematerialized, spiritual form of the subject transfigured by divine grace. The essence of what is being communicated in icons of the saints for example is their participation in the divine life; their faces are turned towards the beholder, to enter into communion with them (faces turned sideways often indicates the absence of enlightenment and sanctification, as in the representation of Judas Iscariot); the face and head may be disproportionately large is relation to the rest of the body; eyes and ears are enlarged, while the mouth may be very small and the lips tightly closed, thus conveying a sense of inner watchfulness and attention; eyes often seem to be inward-looking, turned away from the external world of the senses (*see plates 1, 5, 6, 7, 8 and 12*).

Details of posture are also often used to indicate the character of the person represented in the icon; frequently a figure bowed low will indicate profound reverence and humility, and also the glory and dignity of the One before whom the saints bow down in adoration. And the artistic language that is used to represent such figures is also used in depicting the person of Christ. Dionysius of Fourna, for example, comments on the character of the Incarnate Son of God that has to be conveyed through iconography: 'The body of God in human form is three cubits tall; his head is slightly inclined, and is gentleness is particularly apparent . . . His character is simple, like that of a child, to which he was similar when alive, and which is that of perfect man'.[3]

The gesture of the hands in an icon can be very eloquent. Sometimes a very simple gesture of pointing can move our attention to the person or mystery that is at the heart of an icon. Thus, in icons of the Mother of God Hodegitria, (literally, 'She who points the way'), one arm of the Virgin forms a throne for the Son while the other arm and hand direct our attention to that Incarnate Son who is the Way, the Truth and the Life; Mary quite simply points the way to Christ (*see plate 1*). The gesture of pointing is also required in two other common icons. In icons of the Entry of the Mother of God into the Temple, 'Joachim and Anna are behind her, looking at each other, and pointing at her',[4] while in icons of the Presentation of Christ in the Temple, 'the prophetess Anna points out the Christ and holds a scroll with these words, "This Child has created Heaven and Earth".'[5] (Both quotations from Dionysius of Fourna, *see plates 11 and 3*).

Similarly in icons of St John the Evangelist, gesture is important in stressing the way divine truth is mediated to us through the Evangelist and his servant Prochorus (*see plate 6*). The Evangelist is shown seated in a cave; 'he looks behind him up into heaven in ecstasy, with his right hand on his knees and his left stretched out to Prochorus' (Dionysius of Fourna).[6] The profoundly simple gestures and the positioning of the two men stress their positions as enlightened ones through whose work we too can gain access to the heavenly realm.

Further, the manner in which the hand is represented in a gesture of blessing is important for Dionysius of Fourna; his comments in this case are thought by some not to have very ancient authority, but they do show the significance he and others saw in a detail of iconography that had been common for many centuries before him:

> 'When you paint the blessing hand, do not join the three fingers together, but only cross the thumb and the fourth finger; so that the upright finger, that is to say the index finger,

and the bent middle finger denote the name IC since the upright finger denotes the I, and the curved one which is next to it, the C. The thumb and the fourth finger, which are crossed, with the little finger beside it, denote the name XC. Since the oblique part of the fourth finger, from where it meets the middle finger, makes the X sign and the little finger, where it is curved, the C. In this way the name XC is shown, and through the divine providence of the creator of all things the fingers of the hand of mankind are formed in such a way, with neither more nor fewer but as many as are sufficient to signify this name.'[7]

(The letters IC XC are a Greek abbreviation for Jesus Christ — *see plates 14, 15 and 18*).

The hand raised in blessing is often placed close to the heart of the Saviour or the saint represented, and is often turned inward towards the heart rather than outward to the external world (*see plate 2*). Here again by a symbol and gesture we are led into the spirituality of the hesychast tradition where the Name of Jesus Christ is closely linked with the prayer of the heart, particularly in the form of the Jesus Prayer. In such icons other stylistic techniques draw attention to the interior work of prayer and attentiveness that form the route to the transfigured life. The human form may be shown rather like a silhouette, definitely bounded by a restraining outline; by this means we are led to concentrate on the person of Christ or the saint as one who embodies the life of the world to come. Frequently the clothing of the person will indicate a contrast between the outer garment and the inner person enclosed within the garment, leading us to focus on the interior life of the person in the icon (*see plates 5 and 18(i)*). In such a way the icon gently leads us to embark on the prayer of the heart, and forms the door through which we can enter into that interior work.

These icons also indicate the externalization of the fruits of the prayer of the heart. Often the line of the silhouetted body will be broken by the tip of a pen, the edge of a book or scroll that the subject is holding, or by a wide-open hand in a gesture of self-giving (*see plates 5 and 6*); sometimes the figure of Christ or the saint will extend beyond the main surface of the icon on to the outer frame (*see plate 7*). These subtle details which may often pass un-noticed are part of the silent language of icons used by people whose prime task was to engage in the 'science of sciences and art of arts'. In icons such as these one is immediately drawn into the riches of Orthodox spirituality, an externalization of profound spiritual experience, and a means whereby our own experience may be deepened.

Chapter Eight

ICONS AND THEIR ENVIRONMENT

I

In this final chapter we need to return to a consideration of icons in the Orthodox world at large; to look, as it were, not in close-up, as we have been doing in the past chapters, but, by stepping back, see them in the wider context of the wide 'environment' of the Orthodox Churches. And in order to understand this Orthodox 'environment' we can do no better than recall a particular account of an event in the tenth century that was held to have led to the conversion of Russia to the Orthodox Christian faith as reported in the Russian Primary Chronicle. Prince Vladimir of Kiev sent out emissaries on a journey to discover the true religion, the religion that he should adopt for himself and his people. These men experienced the religion and worship of Islam, of parts of Western Christianity, and then arrived in Constantinople. When they experienced the celebration of the liturgy in the great Church of Hagia Sophia they realized they had reached their goal:

> 'We knew not whether we were in heaven or on earth, for surely there is no such splendour or beauty anywhere upon earth. We cannot describe it to you: only this we know, that God dwells there among men, and that their service surpasses the worship of all other paces. For we cannot forget that beauty.'[1]

And so the faith, worship, beauty and spirituality of Byzantine Orthodoxy was adopted in the year 988 by Prince Vladimir and his people, and found its way into the next thousand years of Russian life and culture.

The Russian emissaries stressed beauty as a powerful part of what they had experienced in Constantinople. For the

Byzantine Christians beauty was an integral part of the faith and life they experienced. Beauty is an expression of the sense of harmony, balance, poise, and integration that is close to the heart of the Orthodox faith. Light, colour and optics, mathematics, geometry and architecture, sound and music, and the theological learning of dogma and spirituality were all integrated to create a harmonious environment within which man could fulfil his destiny. For the Orthodox, beauty is a vital part of the world and of the life of the Church. 'We cannot forget that beauty' is a phrase which echoes in the mind of many who enter into the world of Orthodox spirituality; the beauty lies in both the externals of the Churches and the liturgy, and also in the inner life and holiness of the saints; the sense of beauty is linked to a sense of integration and an inner harmony that inspires, attracts and transforms.

In the liturgy there is a strong sense that God has counted us worthy to share in the glory of Christ. In spite of human sin, God has not abandoned his creation, and the purpose of the Incarnation is that man may come to share in the Divine nature. God is the 'Lover of mankind', to whom the Church gives glory on account of our experience of divine grace and mercy:

> 'We thank thee, master, lover of mankind, thou benefactor of our souls, for that thou hast accounted us this day to be worthy of thine immortal heavenly mysteries.'[2]

Orthodox worship is faithful to the dimension of hope and gratitude that is there in the New Testament, where Christians are spoken of as those who share 'in the glory that is to be revealed', because God has called them 'to his eternal glory in Christ' (1 Peter 5.1,10).

We come to know God through his divine energies, and an important distinction is made in Orthodox theology between the divine essence and the divine energies. The divine essence means the unknowable ground of divinity; the divine energies are those aspects of the divine life that are directed away from the Godhead itself, like rays emanating from the sun. It is through the divine energies that the act of creation is accomplished, and that God is revealed and known as the Holy Trinity.

'We know our God from his energies, but we do not claim that we can draw near to his essence. For his energies come down to us, but his essence remains unapproachable.'[3]

This theological attitude both preserves the transcendence and unknowability of God, while at the same time asserting the reality of his presence in and through his creation. Thus the whole created order is seen as the work of the Holy Trinity, an expression of the Godhead's will and purpose, in which spirit, flesh and matter have their own capacity to mediate the divine energies and love.

The goal of human life is that man should come to union with God, to what Orthodox theologians call 'deification'. This term implies the full perfection of our humanity as through grace we come to share in the divine life of the Holy Trinity. Man is made in the image of God, and called to share in the divine likeness. The image of God in man which was defaced by sin and the fall of man has been restored through the Incarnation of the Divine Son; by Baptism we share once again in the divine image through our incorporation into Christ, and the goal of our discipleship is that we should become like him; thus the work of deification is a supernatural vocation which begins in this life and embraces all aspects of our humanity, and its completion is something we look forward to in heaven.

Beauty, glory, co-operation with the divine energies and sharing in the divine life — these form part of the setting within which icon painters do their work. The icons are created in this environment of faith and worship, and it is to that same environment that they make their particular contribution.

II

Icons were never intended to be museum pieces or regarded as 'works of art'; they were painted to become part of the 'equipment' of an Orthodox church or household. Orthodox church buildings, more than most Western churches, are intended to embody and symbolize a series of relationships. As places of worship they are meeting points for God and man, points where man can enter into the sphere of divine revelation. The emissaries of Prince Vladimir did not know if they were in heaven or on earth when they experienced the liturgy in the largest and most impressive church of the Orthodox world, But most of the older Orthodox churches are small, and very much rooted to the earth. But external size and impressiveness are virtually irrelevant, as the main purpose is to form a gateway into another world. Within the church, the domes and roofs symbolize heaven itself, with representations of Christ in majesty, the Mother of God, and the saints; scenes from the life and ministry of Christ form a bridge between the earthly worshippers and the heavenly realms, and the saints all have their particular part to play. The church building is thus a meeting point of heaven and earth, an embodiment and re-statement of that union of God and man established in the Incarnation; it is the place where the heavenly realm lies open to human access, providing ways and means to take man through into the divine presence and glory.

By the end of the ninth century, when the Church had emerged from the period of the Iconoclast controversy and the place of icons in the life of the Church had been vindicated, the arrangement of church decorations began to follow a common scheme. In the top part of the dome is the figure of Christ Pantocrator — the Lord of the Universe (sometimes with the Mother of God, St John the Fore-runner and angels nearby); beneath the Pantocrator in the drum of the dome are the prophets, and beneath them in the pendentives are the figures of the four Evangelists. In the vaults of the church roof the twelve major Feasts are represented, and beneath these come scenes from the Gospels — illustrating Christ's life and ministry. At the lowest level the frescoes include the great 'warrior saints' like St Demetrius, St George and St Theodore, who by their triumphant spiritual warfare provide examples and encouragement to the Church Militant on earth. This scheme varies according to the size, importance and design of a church, (and is obviously different in a church of the basilica type) but the principles involved remain constant: the earthly Church is the recipient of revelation from the Pantocrator mediated through the prophets, evangelists, and teachers of previous generations; it receives inspiration from the contemplation of the earthly life of Christ; and it engages in prayer and worship in union with the saints and the whole Mystical Body of Christ.

Within the sanctuary the frescoes or mosaics represent another consistent range of themes. The Divine Liturgy is represented, with Christ giving the sacred elements to the Apostles; beneath this are the great Doctors of the Church — St Basil the Great, St Gregory Nazianzen, St John Chrystostom and St Athanasius the Great — shown as participating in the celebration of the liturgy. Over the apse the Mother of God is represented, with her arms held out in prayer and with the figure of Christ against her chest, or else enthroned and holding the incarnate Son; this figure of the Mother of God forms a link between the roof of the church and the lower walls of the apse, symbolizing the role of the Theotokos in linking heaven and earth in the Incarnation. The Mother of God is often referred to as the Ladder or the Bridge, the means whereby God enters into human life and man is led from earth to heaven. This particular theme is often developed in the imagery of funerary chapels.

If the goal of our life is deification and entry into the glory and love of the Holy Trinity through the work of Christ, then those who have already attained that goal have a particularly important part to play in the Church's life and liturgy. The iconostatis or icon screen which marks off the altar (sanctuary) from the main body of the church symbolizes the integration of the earthly worshippers with the whole company of heaven. Beyond the screen, where the sacred elements are consecrated, is the holy of holies, and the movement of priests and other ministers back and forth through the iconostatis between the altar and the nave emphasizes the bonds which the New Covenant has established between heaven and earth. The iconostatis is in theory a link rather than a barrier, but in some instances it does effectively separate the congregation in the nave from the liturgical action in the sanctuary.

There is considerable variation in the scope and size of iconostases; in early churches the screen may be quite modest, while in many later churches in Russia especially the iconostatis reaches from the ground almost to the roof of the church. On the 'royal doors' in the centre of an iconostatis the main themes represented are the Annunciation, the four Evangelists, and St Basil the Great and St John Chrystostom. To either side of the royal doors one can expect to find icons of the Mother of God and Christ, or the saint or mystery to which the particular church is dedicated. Above the doors is the 'deesis group' of icons — Christ in Majesty flanked by the Mother of God and St John the Baptist, the Archangels Michael and Gabriel and other saints. This group shows the saints and archangels as intercessors, aiding the Church on earth with their prayers. Above the deesis group is the row of icons of the twelve major feasts of the Church; and above this are the Old Testament kings and prophets with the icon of Our Lady of the Sign in the centre, representing the fulfilments of Isaiah's prophecy that the Emmanuel would be born of a pure Virgin.

Thus, within an Orthodox church building there is a visual setting forth of the events and the faith that are celebrated in the liturgy. The building itself, with its order and harmony, forms a microcosm of the Cosmos, and within that microcosm the earthly Church celebrates the liturgy in which it is united with the heavenly workshop of the angels and the saints; man in Christ takes his place in the harmony, balance, joy, beauty and holiness of the redeemed creation. In the liturgy, the icons are important as representing or making present a particular saint or mystery. For Orthodox Christians, a liturgy without icons would be tantamount to separating the Church on earth from the Church in heaven — a denial of the very work of Christ which the liturgy celebrates. The icons and frescoes of an Orthodox church building create a powerful sense that here in the Church and its liturgy is the point where we may experience the glory of God and receive the fulness of divine grace.

The emissaries of Prince Vladimir could not put into words the beauty they had experienced: 'Only this we know, that God dwells there among men'. Their comment sums up the essence of the Orthodox faith in the Word made flesh, in Christ as Emmanuel, 'God with us'. To the great theologians of the fourth century like St Gregory of Nyssa and St Gregory Nazianzen man's true dignity lies in the way he is created to belong to both the world of matter and the world of mind; in man alone do mind and matter interpenetrate, and through man, matter is taken up into the praise and glory of God through worship and the activity of Christ and his Church. The Word made flesh restores man to his true dignity and vocation, and as man enters into the realm of grace through Baptism and the Eucharist, so he is transformed into the image and likeness of him who is the true image of the invisible God, Emmanuel, God with us.

At the heart of the Church's annual cycle of liturgical celebration is the Passion and Resurrection of Christ (*see plates 14, 15 and 18(ii)*). In celebrating the resurrection the Church is not only looking to a past event, but sharing in a living reality: the Risen Christ present with his Church, leading us to our true destiny in heaven. In Orthodoxy, the cosmic implications of the Resurrection are stressed by the teaching about the transformed nature of the resurrection body of Christ, and by the doctrine of the harrowing of hell, by which those who died before Christ are brought within the scope of his victorious work of redemption. If the Resurrection is celebrated as the final conquest of sin and death and the opening up of Paradise, then other events prior to the Resurrection are seen by the Orthodox Church as preludes to the full glory of the Resurrection. The Transfiguration of Christ on Mount Tabor (*see plate 16*) was a revelation to Peter, James and John of the divine glory of the Incarnate Son. In that incident the disciples perceive not only the humanity of the Christ they have known and loved, but also the truth of his divine nature. To them is given a foretaste of the divine glory that is to be later manifested in its fulness in the Resurrection. Again, at Christ's Baptism we are told that the heavens were opened and the Spirit descended on him in the form of a dove; once more we have the imagery of that bond between heaven and earth that is given in Christ; Heaven is no longer closed to man, and man, in the person of Jesus Christ, is open to the grace and power of the Spirit of God. Icons of the Baptism of Christ (*see plate 10*) powerfully convey the sense of the divine spirit descending into the human realm as Christ is baptized in the Jordan by John the Baptist. Prior to the Resurrection, Transfiguration and the Baptism of Christ is the mystery of the Incarnation itself (*see plate 9*). In the icons which are related to this mystery, the Blessed Virgin Mary has a prominent place; incidents from both the canonical and the apocryphal Gospels (especially the so-called Protevangelium of James) are used to create an iconographic sequence showing her conception, birth, presentation in the Temple, and Annunciation, prior to the Nativity of the Saviour himself.

The Church Feasts' sequence in the iconostatis includes icons of the Virgin's Birth, Presentation, Annunciation and Assumption, icons of the Lord's Nativity, Presentation, Baptism, Transfiguration, Entry into Jerusalem, Resurrection and Ascension, and icons of Pentecost and the Exaltation of the Cross, (this latter feast, celebrated on 14 September, originated as a commemoration of the dedication of the basilica of the Resurrection in Jerusalem in 335, and soon became linked with the discovery of the true Cross, and its recovery in 629 from the Persians who had taken possession of it in 614. The feast of the Exaltation of the Cross is a celebration of the significance of the Cross of Christ as the source of life and wisdom, and victory over the powers of evil). Other icons frequently included in this sequence are the Raising of Lazarus, the Crucifixion, and the women bearing spices at the tomb of Christ. The arrangement of these icons is usually according to the annual cycle of the festivals in the Christian Year. This important part of the iconostasis holds before the eye throughout the year the events and the dogmatic truths of the Church's teaching that are given individual special attention on their particular feast days. Thus these icons help to anchor individual Christian spirituality to the liturgy and to the revelation given within the

Church. The spirituality of the individual Christ is built up within and from the life of the Body of Christ; and the individual icons are generally created to take their part in the harmony and beauty of the whole composition that makes up the interior of an Orthodox church.

III

Church buildings form the most obvious environment for most icons; but the wider environment of Orthodox society must not be overlooked. In the Byzantine Empire great buildings of importance to Church and State reflected the same political and spiritual convictions that the earthly life of human society is integrally linked with the spiritual realm, and that Christ is the Lord of the Universe in all its diverse aspects. The same convictions and sacral structure of society are evident in Constantinople, and in the lesser centres of Imperial power; for example, at Ravenna in Nothern Italy (from where the western half of the Empire was administered at the time of Justinian), or at Mistra, in the Peloponnese (an important Byzantine outpost in the Palaeologue period). In Moscow, the cathedrals in the Kremlin witness to the continuance of the Byzantine type of theocracy on Russian territory; and outside the Kremlin stands the Cathedral of St Basil, built by Ivan the Terrible to celebrate the victory over the Tartars at a time when Muscovite power was at its height and linked to an essentially theocratic view of the role of the Grand Prince.

Two further examples of the integral relation between the spiritual and the secular in respect to the setting within which icons were cherished should also be considered. As mentioned in chapter three, at major developments in the history of the Russian state, the presence of the icon of Our Lady of Vladimir at the centre of power was regarded as essential; thus the icon was housed at Kiev, at Vladimir and finally in 1395 Moscow. Its fate and location were considered to be bound up with the fate and destiny of the Russian people. Other examples of the real power that icons were thought to possess can be taken from any century of the history of the

Orthodox Church; as an example we can look at a favourite theme among icon painters in Novgorod during the fifteenth century, the battle between the Novgorodians and the Suzdalians, the Suzdalians representing the rising Muscovite power against which the Novgorodians held out until 1478, when their city was annexed to the domain of Ivan III, Grand Prince of Moscow. Earlier in the proud history of 'Lord Novgorod the Great', as the republican city was known, Prince Andrei Bogolyubskiy had beseiged Novgorod with his Suzdalian troops in 1169; the Suzdalian forces were repelled, according to the legend, by the heavenly assistance of Saints Boris, Gleb, George and Demetrius of Thessalonica who were sent by the Virgin to aid the Novgorodians who were under her protection; the icon of Our Lady of the Sign taken from the Church of the Saviour in Il'yin Street was believed to be a powerful element in the spiritual armoury by which the Suzdalians were repulsed.

The concerns of this world and its political developments are equally part of the environment in which icons were created and used. This can be further illustrated by the range of patron saints who are represented in icons. St Nicholas (*see plate 7*) and St George, for example, had an almost universal appeal; St Cosmos and St Damian are honoured as healers throughout the Orthodox world; in Russia, devotion to St Blasius as a protector of animals took over from the cult of the local Slav deity Veles; and at a yet more local level a popular cult in the Novgorod area was the devotion to St Florus and St Laurus, patrons of horse-breeding. Such cults and their associated icons, as well as the frequent way-side shrines to the Virgin Mother of God reveal the homely concern for the sanctification of the whole of human life that is there within the ethos of Orthodoxy. In one sense the holiness or other-worldliness of God and the spiritual dimension of life are enshrined within the icons; but equally there is the homeliness that sees God and the saints as concerned with ordinary life and its problems. At all levels — the artistic, the spiritual, the political and the domestic — icons reveal a profound concern for the integration and inter-relationship of the spiritual and the material, the sacred and the secular.

This is seen at its most domestic level in the household shrines where icons form the focal point of devotion for individuals and families within the home. This can be seen in any devout Orthodox household today, and many examples can be found in literature that comes from an Orthodox background. In chapter four of *My Childhood*, for example, Maxim Gorky tells of some of his memories of the religious background of his grandparents' home. His Grandfather was very stern, but his Grandmother showed much warmth, love, and profound religious devotion:

> 'I liked Grandmother's God very much, as he was so near to her and I often used to ask her:
> "Tell me about God!"
> When she talked about God, heaven or the angels she grew smaller and more gentle, her face regained its youth and her moist eyes radiated a particularly warm light. I took the heavy locks of her hair in my hands and wound them round my neck. All ears, I would sit quite still as I listened to her endless stories that never once bored me.
> "Man can't see God — if he did, he'd go blind. Only the Saints can look him full in the face."
> To see her wipe the dust from the icons and clean the chasubles was both an interesting and a pleasant experience. The icons were very rich, with pearls, silver and coloured stones along their edges. She would nimbly pick an icon up, smile at it and say with great feeling:
> "What a lovely little face!"
> Then she would cross herself and kiss the icon.
> Often, it seemed, she played at icons like my crippled cousin Katerina played with her dolls, seriously and with deep emotion.'[4]

IV

Church buildings, Imperial palaces, and peasant houses — these are all equally part of the environment of icons; and the icons form part of the environment in which a monastic spiritual master, a Byzantine or Russian Emperor, a Greek or Russian peasant, and any other Orthodox Christian fulfil their spiritual vocation according to their perception of the

Orthodox way. This rich inheritance of the Orthodox Church is steadily becoming more available to us in the West; it is an inheritance of Christian spirituality and art which many Western Christians find highly significant as we face the dilemmas and tensions that are so deeply rooted within the Western Churches and Western societies. The holy icons form one important starting point for the exploration of this inheritance, for the icons cannot be understood apart from the faith they enshrine and represent; they form part of the visual language of Orthodoxy; and like the verbal language of the Church, this visual language is there to lead us from the beauty of what can be seen and heard with the senses, to the Beauty and Goodness of the Invisible God who has been revealed in his perfect Image and Likeness, Jesus Christ.

Appendix

THE PAINTING OF ICONS
by Richard Temple

I

A certain amount of confusion exists regarding knowledge of the techniques and methods of icon painting. This is partly due to the fact that no ancient accounts of icon painting exist. The Russian *Stroganov Painters Handbook* dates from the late nineteenth century and the *Painter's Manual* of Dionysius of Fourna, found on Mount Athos, is no earlier than the late eighteenth century, though it is considered to incorporate some instructions from older books on which the author drew. In our own times something of a false mystique has been generated by so-called icon painting schools or courses given today where the 'genuine old methods' are taught. These methods, when they are genuine, are nineteenth century and perpetuate techniques that were introduced after the sixteenth century in the period which purists would consider decadent.

Icon painting today is a lost art and even by the late eighteenth century was hopelessly compromised by the influences of Western painting. But in the antique and medieval periods icon painters achieved a mastery over the materials with which they worked which, by the standards of the last two hundred years, defies comprehension and at which we can only wonder.

Tenth century theologians stated that icon painting was an actual *spiritualisation of matter*, a re-enactment of the Incarnation, reflecting actually and not only symbolically the appearance of God at the human and earthly level. Incorporated into this teaching were fragments of an ancient knowledge, elaborated by Plato and the neo-platonists, about the nature of matter and the substance and structure of the

99

universe. Techniques of painting were developed in the light of such ideas. This means that the great masters of icon painting had an understanding of the materials with which they worked that we can only approach today through microscopy, spectroscopy, analysis of molecular structure, analysis of atomic structure, radiation discharge measurement, indices of light refraction and other scientific technical aids. But our scientific methods can only divide and subdivide; we try to reach truth by reduction, whereas the great icon painters were spiritual masters who achieved a psychical state of inner unity, combining in themselves both divine and earthly energies whose actions gave access to a comprehensive and whole truth. Any gesture, any physical undertaking, when carried out in the light of this special state, would be bound to communicate itself to vegetable and mineral material substances whose qualities and vibrations would inevitably be harmonised by the influence of a man imbued with divine energies. To paint an icon is to bring about a transformation of matter that is only real as a result of a transformation in the inner being of the painter.

That is why it is necessary to look carefully at certain early icons, such as those of Andrei Rublev in Russia, or some Byzantine icons in Greece. Such works of art provide a glimpse down an immensely long corridor of time, showing us a period of a thousand years — from the sixth century to the sixteenth century — when sacred paintings were a continuous and living tradition. The antiquity of this tradition is as striking in its adherence to the technical methods of the craft as the continuity of the iconographic principle itself. The origins of the craft are roughly contemporary with the historical period of the Gospels.

II

Quite a number of panel paintings have survived from the late Graeco-Roman period. They are commonly known as Fayum portraits because most of them were found at the settlement of that name in Hellenistic times at the mouth of the Nile Delta in Egypt. These paintings are all funeral portraits and are often extraordinarily beautiful. We know little about the religion of the group who lived at Fayum between the first century BC and the third century AD, but their paintings are obviously descended from the masks moulded in relief on mummy cases of the earlier Pharaonic period.

Fayum portraits were approximately life-size heads, naturalistically painted, but with spiritually idealised youthful looks. They were done on thin wooden panels that were inserted, over the face of the deceased person, at the surface of the mummy case. One, in the British Museum, has a drip of paint on the bottom edge in a place that would not normally be seen since it would have been under the binding that held it in place. From the angle of the fall of the drip it is concluded that the painting was done with the panel in an upright position. In other words the Fayum portraits were the first easel paintings as well as being the immediate forerunners of the first icons.

The earliest icons that we know come from St Catherine's Monastery on Mount Sinai and other places in Egypt. They date from the late fifth and sixth centuries and are closely similar in style to the Fayum portraits; although the content has changed, passing from pagan mystery to Christian image, the technique at least is the same: wax encaustic. This means that the colours, derived mostly from mineral sources, were held together in a medium of wax.

Opinions vary on exactly how the pigments were mixed in the medium and how they were applied to the picture surface. In any case we can be sure that the wax was hot and therefore molten while it was being worked. Also it is fairly certain that spatulas were used, but whether instead of brushes or in conjunction with them is not sure.

Wax encaustic was the universally established technique employed throughout the Christian world during the first iconographical period which lasted for at least three hundred years until the iconoclast war in the eighth century.

Iconoclasm was finally overcome at the end of the ninth century and with the next period of iconography came the technique of using egg instead of wax with which to bind the colours. Icon painting continued with the egg tempera method up until modern times and has never accepted oils as a medium.

In egg tempera painting the pigments are held in a medium of egg yolk mixed with, or tempered by, water. It is quick to dry and gives a smooth, hard, translucent finish. It is a more difficult technique to learn than oil painting and it is applied, not to canvas, but to a hard and polished plaster surface.

We usually give this surface its Italian name, 'gesso'. It is made of finely ground chalk whiting, sometimes with marble and sometimes even, for the very finest icons, alabaster ground into a fine powder; this is mixed with size and applied to a wooden panel. It is then rubbed and burnished to achieve the smoothest possible surface.

Thus there are three basic elements in the structure of an icon. Firstly, the wooden board or panel, technically known as the support; secondly, the prepared gesso surface; thirdly the medium and pigments. However there are many additions and refinements to these basic elements.

The panel support would be shaped and treated in ways that took into account the inevitable processes of ageing. For example it was usual, from the earliest times, to strengthen the panel by sticking down strips of linen in places where it might be liable to split or crack. Cross-grained strips of wood were nailed or slotted onto the back for the same reason and also in order to prevent warping.

In many icons it is apparent that the gesso is sometimes more than a millimetre in thickness. But it was put on in many separate layers; fifteen or twenty would not be unusual. In wealthy institutions a layer of gold leaf would be laid on this gesso and burnished with an agate stone. The gold leaf would not be laid directly onto the gesso but onto a special preparation called bole made from red or yellow earth.

Finally the surface would be protected from the atmosphere by various glazes performing a similar function to varnish.

A typical cross section of a fifteenth century icon might look something like this:

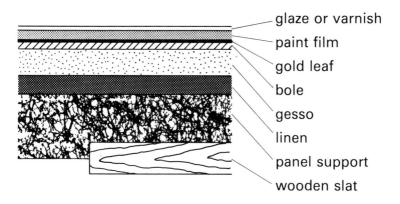

glaze or varnish
paint film
gold leaf
bole
gesso
linen
panel support
wooden slat

III

There is something magical about the colours in old icons. They were ground by hand, of course, and mostly derived from minerals. Some of these, like azurite which was used for blue, were easily and almost universally found while lapis lazuli, which came from Persia only, was not only rare but extremely costly. To the unspoilt medieval eye colour was always a rare and precious commodity which, apart from flora and minerals produced by nature, could only be manufactured by man at great expense and with great labour and skill. Colour was not part of everyday life but an attribute of wealth and power, which were themselves attributes of religion and superior knowledge.

The knowledge associated with colour and techniques of art in the early Christian period was of a high order. It derived from the philosophical teachings of the neo-platonists who described the universe as irradiated with energy from the Divine Realm of which the *symbol*, in the physical world, was light. The breaking up of light into colour, its constituent elements, symbolised the principle of unity within multiplicity. Such schools of knowledge continued to exist even after the fall of Constantinople, as the art of Andrei Rublev and his school testifies. But after the beginning of the sixteenth century the knowledge gradually disappears. The techniques and the elaborate traditions of the craft were to remain for at least another century but maintained through inertia; and from the seventeenth century until the end of the nineteenth century the old methods were gradually and imperceptibly worn away until almost entirely replaced by Western techniques.

This is why the dating of icons is so important. The vast majority of icons that we see today are later than the fifteenth century and consequently their quality is measured by their distance in time from the source.

There are many variations in technique during the long decadence of icon painting. These are mainly associated with composition, which tended to become crowded; with forms, which tended to become either naturalistic or rigid; and with colour which tended to become dull and inharmonious.

Another tendency during this period was for icon painting to become folkloric and popular. Such art can have great charm for us today and often, especially in Russia, retains some of the innocence and purity of vision characteristic of the earlier periods. The conservative nature of provincial attitudes was often a guarantee, to some extent, of the continuation of authentic traditions of technique even if the level of artistry was inferior.

Often the palette was surprisingly limited. Coming from many poor country churches we find beautiful icons whose range and variety of colours comes almost entirely from the earths: from brilliant yellow ochre to the deepest and most sombre red ochre. Combinations from within this range produce great variety of colour and, with the admixture of black (burnt bones) and white (white lead), come new and wide-ranging tonalities of greens and greys.

But in the great centres of learning in the period up to the fifteenth century Byzantine and Slav painters achieved a mastery over colour that not even the Impressionists surpassed. Such theories as the 'law of complementary tones' were fully understood and the most dazzling and brilliant effects of colour were achieved from such materials as *lapis lazuli*, which we have mentioned, *terre verte*, and the 'flaming vermillion' made from mercuric sulphide. The suspension of such colours in the egg medium and laid over a gesso or gilt-gesso ground, allowed the light to pass through the materials and be reflected into the eye in a series of events that are almost alchemical in that they demonstrate a transformation of matter, or rather, of vibrations of light. The transformation of matter by the finer vibrations of light can be regarded as more than the ultimate spiritual symbol: it is a demonstration of the actions of divine energy manifested on the physical plane.

PLATE 1 *(opposite)*

THE SMOLENSK MOTHER OF GOD

Russian; sixteenth century.

'Hodigitria is the name given to a style of icon in which the right hand of the Virgin points to the Incarnate Son of God who sits enthroned on her left arm, facing out from the icon with a scroll in his left hand and the right hand raised in blessing. The Son in the arms of his Mother is not shown as an infant, but as the 'pre-eternal God' and incarnate Wisdom who has come into the world, and who has the divine authority to bless and instruct. In this style of icon any expression of tenderness between Mother and Son is severely curtailed, and the Mother is the 'one who points the way', the guide who points away from herself to her Son (John 2.5). She has a quiet contemplative gaze of inward attentiveness, knowledge and love, drawing the beholder into the mystery of the divine presence that is manifested in the Son she presents to the world. In this icon there is a subtle balance between the inwardness of the Virgin's attitude, and the external presentation of the Son whose figure breaks the line of the silhouette of the Virgin. The terms 'Mother of God' and 'Theotokos' (God-bearer) stress the reality of the Incarnation: the divinity as well as the humanity of the Incarnate Son.

The Hodigitria style of icon became clearly elaborated in the ninth century, and became a major Byzantine type of icon; there were prototypes going back to sixth century Syria (and according to tradition, right back to St Luke); a considerable range of developments took place once this style entered Russia. The Smolensk Mother of God derives from a Hodgitria icon placed in Smolensk Cathedral in 1101.

In this style of icon, truths about the incarnation are expressed, but the Mother of God also stands before us as a symbol and type of the Church and the Christian vocation: to point away from self to Christ, and yet to have an inner awareness of his presence in ourselves through the life of prayer and worship. He is the incarnate Wisdom, the Way, the Truth and the Life (John 14. 6); the Virgin and the Church point to Him with gentleness, love, firmness and inner conviction.

PLATE 2 *(opposite)*
CHRIST PANTOCRATOR
Novgorod School; fifteenth century.

This icon shows Christ enthroned as the all-ruling Lord of the universe. Within the oval mandorla are the Cherubim surrounding the enthroned figure of Christ, while in the four corners of the icon are the symbols of the Evangelists (the bottom left figure is missing through damage to the icon) with rays of light reaching them from the central figure of Christ. Christ's right hand is raised in a gesture of blessing that is turned towards the heart, indicating the inner knowledge in Christ that is given outward expression in the open book. Both the book and the gesture of blessing help to make the icon a very welcoming one. The balance of contrasting colours, and the combination of geometrical shapes (two rectangles, two ovals, and one diamond shape) give a sense of balance and harmony to the whole composition. The oval as a symbol of the union of heaven and earth, spirit and matter, draws our attention in to the central figure with its great sense of poise and dignity, while the rays of light emanating to the symbols of the Evangelists indicate the outward movement of the divine energies and revelation.

The texts often printed on the book in Christ's hand in this type of icon include:

> 'Do not judge by appearances . . . but judge with right judgement.' (John 7.24)
> 'Come to me all who labour and are heavy laden, and I will give you rest . . . For my yoke is easy, and my burden is light.' (Matt. 11.28,30)

Sometimes the Pantocrator figure of Christ is portrayed as the stern Judge who is Lord of the universe, and to whom we must all render account. The Pantocrator figure is common inside the domes of Orthodox churches, and also as part of the Deesis group of an iconostasis.

Where Christ is represented as the Pantocrator, the letters IC XC are near the figure of Christ; and, to emphasise his cosmic role rather than the incarnation, the Greek letters for 'The One' are inscribed in the halo around Christ's head, as in this icon, and as in plate 17.

> 'He is the image of the invisible God, the first-born of all creation; for in him all things were created, in heaven and on earth, visible and invisible . . . all things were created through him and for him. He is before all things, and in him all things hold together.' (Col. 1.15–17)
> 'None but Jesus Christ himself, unifier of what is disunited, can give your heart lasting peace from passions.' (St Hesychios the Priest)[1]

PLATE 3 *(opposite)*

DEESIS

Russian; fifteenth century.

The Deesis composition first appears in the Comnene era of the Byzantine Empire (1081–118), and stresses the role of the saints, especially the Mother of God and St John the Baptist, in interceding for humanity at the judgement seat of Christ. The word Deesis means prayer, and later Deesis compositions in Russian iconostases were extended to include archangels and many saints gathered in intercession around the central figure of the Christ Pantocrator.

In this small panel icon Christ is in the centre, raised up from the lowest levels on a throne and footstool; in his left hand is the book — the external manifestation of Wisdom, and at the same time the means whereby we are invited to enter into the wisdom of the heart in Christ; the right hand is turned inward in blessing. On either side of Christ stand the Mother of God and St John the Baptist, the God-bearer and the Forerunner, each with their empty hands outstretched in prayer, interceding for humanity to the Christ who came to redeem the world, and in whose plan of salvation they each had a central part to play.

PLATE 4 *(opposite)*

THE HOLY TRINITY

Moscow School; early sixteenth century.

Icons of the Holy Trinity are particularly associated with the feast of Pentecost; this is the time when the Church celebrates the outpouring of the Holy spirit on the Apostles and the beginning of the Church's mission; it is also the point at which the revelation of the Holy Trinity has been accomplished. Thus, for the Orthodox Churches, it is not only a celebration of the outpouring of the Spirit, but, like the Baptism of the Lord, a celebration of the revelation of the central Christian dogma of the Holy Trinity. The feast which celebrates the fulfilment of Christ's promise of the gift of the Holy Spirit also brings to fulfilment the promises given in the Old Testament to 'Abraham and his seed'. Thus it is fitting that the icon of the Holy Trinity approved by the Orthodox Church should use elements from the revelation given in the Old Testament to be the vehicle by which the fuller revelation of the New Testament is given visual expression.

The early Fathers of the Church saw the incident described in Genesis 18 as a foreshadowing of the later revelation of the Holy Trinity. The Lord appears to Abraham by the oak of Mamre, and Abraham sees three men to whom he gives hospitality. The 'hospitality of Abraham' is seen as a meeting of God and Abraham, and by the late fourth century the theme is found in wall paintings and soon becomes a common theme in Christian art.

For about a thousand years the visual representation of this theme included the three visitors shown as winged beings to represent their heavenly nature, the figures of Abraham and Sarah, the table, the oak of Mamre, the home of Abraham and Sarah, and sometimes a servant killing a calf, and other illustrative details. In the early fifteenth century, probably between 1408 and 1425, Andrei Rublev, a monk at the monastery of the Holy Trinity some miles north of Moscow, painted the now world famous icon of the Holy Trinity which is exhibited in the Tretyakov Gallery in Moscow. In this icon Rublev drastically reduced the traditional details associated with this theme, and concentrated on the figures of the three angels. Abraham, Sarah, servants and other details are removed; the home of Abraham and Sarah and oak of Mamre are reduced to symbols alongside the very distorted mountain peak, and the focus of attention is the three angels grouped around the table, with the chalice of sacrifice in the centre. Rublev's whole composition is

Continued on page 142

PLATE 5 *(opposite)*
ST MARK
Byzantine, from Cyprus; late fourteenth century.

This icon belongs to the tradition of Byzantine painting that was influenced by the great revival of spirituality and art under the Paleologue Emperors; some of the best examples of work in this tradition can be seen in the Kariye Camii (Our saviour in Chora) in Istanbul, where the mosaics (c.1320; *see plate 18*) have a remarkable warmth and vitality that combine interest in human and environmental detail with the authentic spiritual purpose of icon painting.

In this icon of St Mark we see the saint depicted as one in whom mind and heart are united in knowledge and prayer; the enlarged neck that unites the head and the body helps to create an impression of unity and harmony within the saint. The sense of inner tranquility is enhanced by the strong line of the silhouette which encloses the figure; this line is only broken by the tip of the pen — which thus forms the link between the inner world of the saint's spiritual knowledge and experience, and the outer world of external communication by the written and spoken word. The pen — which seems to float in its position rather than being held in the saint's fingers — also points to the heart, and helps to create a close inter-relationship within the icon between the inwardness expressed in the gaze of the eyes, the heart as the centre of knowledge and motivation, and the book as the outward expression of spiritual truth. The saint's outer garment enfolds his body, but also helps to lead our attention on to the inner reality of the saint's life, the interior life of prayer and attentiveness.

The following quotations are a verbal expression of the spirituality that is given visual expression in this icon:

> 'He who dwells continually within his own heart is detached from the attractions of the world, for he lives in the Spirit and cannot know the desires of the flesh.' (St Diadochos of Photiki)[3]
> 'Be attentive to yourself, so that nothing destructive can separate you from the love of God. Guard your heart, and do not grow listless.' (St Isaiah the Solitary)[4]
> 'Extreme watchfulness and the Prayer of Jesus Christ, undistracted by thoughts, are the necessary basis for inner vigilance and unfathomable stillness of soul.' (St Hesychios the Priest)[5]

PLATE 6 *(opposite)*

ST JOHN THE EVANGELIST

Moscow School c.1500.
From a set of icons of the four Evangelists on the Royal Doors of an iconostasis.

This is an excellent example of the way icons can speak eloquently by their stillness and silence.

St John is shown as an old man passing on the revelation he receives to his scribe Prochorus. St John looks up to the left behind him (Rev. 1.10–11), and the gestures of both hands point across to Prochorus. Prochorus is seated in front of the cave — the symbol of ignorance and unredeemed humanity — waiting to receive the revelation that is given through the Evangelist. The strong downward diagonal movement from the segment of the celestial sphere in the top left corner to the stool of Prochorus in the bottom right corner is balanced and held in tension by the large figure of St John facing the smaller figure of Prochorus, and by the diagonal movement from the stool in the bottom left corner to the mountain top in the upper right hand corner. The mountains which form the background help to balance the composition, and also remind us of the spiritual nature of the whole composition *(see pp.34 and 83)* Both the figures are raised on stools, again emphasizing that they have been raised above the merely material level of life through the revelation they have received.

The silhouette of the figures is only broken by the hand of St John and the scroll of Prochorus, two small details which help to create the sense of communication between the spiritual master and his disciple. The small mouth, the attentive eyes and ear, and the whole posture of St John help to create a sense of profound humility and interior love that is open to receive the divine revelation and to pass it on to those with the same diligence, attentiveness, humility and willingness to learn that is shown in the posture of Prochorus.

> 'He who has achieved stillness has arrived at the very centre of the mysteries.' (St John Climacus)[6]
> 'When the heart has acquired stillness it will perceive the heights and depths of knowledge; the ear of the still intellect will be made to hear marvellous things from God.' (St Hesychios the Priest)[7]

PLATE 7 *(opposite)*

ST NICHOLAS

Novgorod School; fifteenth century.

St Nicholas was a fourth century Bishop of Myra in Lycia in Asia Minor. He has been one of the most popular saints in both Eastern and Western Churches. Tradition and legend include some lively exploits by this saint to save those unjustly condemned to death, to rescue sailors in distress, to save girls from prostitution, and to bring to life again three murdered children who had been hidden in a brine tub. It is not surprising that St Nicholas has been seen as patron saint of children, sailors, merchants, etc. And the Russians have a saying: 'If anything happens to God, we have always got St Nicholas'. Many icons of St Nicholas include smaller illustrations around the edge of the icon with scenes from the saint's life to enclose the central portrait of the saint.

In Orthodox tradition, St Nicholas has been honoured as one who exemplifies the pastoral office of a Bishop, as a staunch defender of the Orthodox Faith, and as a man of prayer — particularly as an intercessor. These three central aspects of the saint's life illustrate how his 'love for others' is rooted in his faith and prayer. The legends testify to the conviction that true holiness and prayer are not divorced from the everyday common concerns of humanity.

This icon shows the saint as a man of prayer, as an example of the hesychast traditions of the Desert Fathers and others in that long spiritual tradition that was so important in fifteenth century Russia. The icon does not give us a naturalistic representation of the saint's appearance, but rather a presentation of the inner life of the saint transfigured through the purification of the heart and inner prayer. The 'distortion' of the nose, ears, and cranium should lead us to recognize the non-naturalistic nature of the icon — one which powerfully conveys a sense of inner concentration of spiritual energies in attentiveness and prayer.

> 'Continuity of attention produces inner stability; inner stability produces a natural intensification of watchfulness; and this intensification gradually and in due measure gives contemplative insight into spiritual warfare. This in turn is succeeded by persistence in the Jesus Prayer and by the state that Jesus confers, in which the intellect, free from all images, enjoys complete quietude.' (St Hesychios the Priest)[8]

PLATE 8 *(opposite)*
ST SERGIUS

Moscow School; mid fifteenth century.
Possibly the earliest known icon of St Sergius.

St Sergius was *the* great Russian exemplar of the hesychast spiritual tradition. He embodies the injunction in Psalm 46.10. 'Be still and know that I am God.' As the saint is represented in this icon he is a living expression of profound stillness and knowledge.

> Spiritual knowledge illuminates man through its inner energy, while wisdom does so through being expressed outwardly. Spiritual knowledge comes through prayer, deep stillness and complete detachment, while wisdom comes through humble meditation on Holy Scripture and, above all through grace given by God.' (St Diadochos of Photiki)[9]

The saint's love and humility are the fruit of the inner work of prayer and purification; the posture indicates the 'kenosis' or self-emptying (see Philippians 2.7) which was such a major element in Russian sanctity. The axial symmetry, the unbroken silhouette of the figure of the saint, the placing of the figure within the panel, and the extension of the halo on to the raised edge of the panel all help to create a strong sense of the presence of one whose inner work of prayer has a continuing significance for those who behold this icon.

The hands and the scroll draw attention to the heart, and the inner work of prayer. The small mouth, large ear, and attentive eyes convey a sense of inner attentiveness, stillness, dispassion and love.

The warmth, compassion and tenderness that are conveyed by the icon are both welcoming and challenging, inviting the beholder to tread the same inner path to holiness that St Sergius so eminently exemplified.

PLATE 9 *(opposite)*

THE NATIVITY OF CHRIST (Feast day, 25 December)

Cretan School; early sixteenth century.
The central panel from a triptych.

The Feast of the Nativity of Christ is a celebration of both the Incarnation and the re-creation of the world in Christ. It celebrates the reality of the Incarnation of the eternal Word, the Son of God, and the fact that through this incarnation the world is transfigured and restored. The liturgical texts for the feast show the wealth of implications that are celebrated along with the central events that are remembered.

'Today the Virgin gives birth to Him who is above all being, and the earth offers a cave to Him whom no man can approach.'[10]
'The whole creation is made rich: let it rejoice and be of good cheer. The Master of all has come to live with His servants, and from the bondage of the enemy He delivers us who were made subject to corruption (Rom. 8.20,21). In swaddling clothes and lying in a manger, He is manifest a young child, the pre-eternal God.'[11]

Another text sees the whole creation involved in an act of gratitude and welcome to the Incarnate God:

'What shall we offer Thee, O Christ, who for our sakes hast appeared on earth as man? Every creature made by Thee offers Thee thanks. The angels offer Thee a hymn; the heavens a star; the Magi, gifts; the shepherds, their wonder; the earth, its cave; the wilderness, the manger: and we offer Thee a Virgin Mother. O pre-eternal God, have mercy upon us.'[12]

All this liturgical material is reflected and represented in the icon of the Nativity. The ray of light from the heavenly realm shines over the place of the Incarnation and points directly to the Christ-child who lays in the manger within the cave. The light of the Christ-child shines forth in the darkness of the cave, and disperses the darkness of the shadow of death that covers mankind. The reference to the wilderness in the third text quoted earlier is a reminder that here in the manger is the One who is the Bread of Life, the true Bread from heaven (John 6), given in the Eucharist, and pre-figured in the manna given to the people of Israel in their journey through the wilderness. The ox and the ass in the icon looking down on the Incarnate Lord represent the fulfilment of Isaiah 1.23 'The ox knows its owner and the ass its master's crib' — i.e. the animal creation joins in recognition of the Incarnation of the Son of God.

Continued on page 142

PLATE 10 *(opposite)*
THE BAPTISM OF THE LORD (Feast day, 6 January)
Central Russian; c.1600.

The feast of the Baptism of the Lord is also known in the Orthodox Churches as the Epiphany or the Theophany, since it celebrates the manifestation of Christ and the beginning of his public ministry, and also the revelation of the Holy Trinity through the voice of the Father and the descent of the Holy Spirit on the Incarnate Son who enters the waters of the Jordan.

In this icon Christ stands stripped naked in the waters of the Jordan; the dark cave shape in the centre of the icon emphasizes the humility of the one who empties himself (Phil 2.7) to take the form of a servant and experience human death and burial; with his right hand Christ blesses the waters of the Jordan and sanctifies them by his immersion in them so that the waters of Baptism become for the Church the means of a new birth into the life of Christ. From the left, John the Forerunner baptizes the Lord, while on the right three angels stand in attendance and witness this marvel of humility and revelation. There is a strong axial symmetry in this icon, with the standing figure of Christ occupying the central position. In most icons of the Baptism of the Lord there is at the top a segment of a circle representing the divine realm, and rays descending from it enclosing the form of a dove over the head of Christ; these details not only strengthen the sense of axial symmetry but they also help to convey the theological truths of this feast of the Theophany.

The liturgical texts of the feast celebrate a rich variety of theological and spiritual themes that come together in this festival. The following examples show something of the spiritual significance of this feast to Orthodox Christians and illuminate what we can see in the icons of the feast.

The humility of Christ:

> 'Today Christ has come to be baptized in Jordan; today John touches the head of the Master. The powers of heaven are amazed as they behold the marvellous mystery ... And we who have been enlightened cry aloud: Glory to God made manifest, who has appeared on earth and brought light to the world.'[14]
> 'Wearing the form of a servant, O Christ, thou comest forth to be baptized by a servant in the streams of the Jordan, granting deliverance from the servitude of ancient sin, and sanctifying and enlightening us.'[15]

Continued on page 143

PLATE 11 *(opposite)*

THE PRESENTATION OF CHRIST IN THE TEMPLE
(Feast day, 2 February)

North Russian; end of sixteenth century.

St Luke tells us (2, 22–23) that Mary and Joseph took the child Jesus into the Temple in obedience to the requirements of the Law given in Exodus 13.2 and Leviticus 12.6–8. The details of the visit that St Luke gives us show that he saw this as a meeting of the representatives of the Old Covenant with the Saviour who comes in fulfilment of the promises to Israel and to be the light of revelation for the whole world. The Orthodox Churches often refer to this feast as 'The Meeting of our Lord and Saviour Jesus Christ'. The festival itself seems to have been observed since the late fourth century, and the iconography associated with the feast developed from the fifth century onwards.

This icon with its harmonious balance of the figures involved emphasises the meeting of the devout Simeon and Anna with the Child brought into the Temple by Mary and Joseph. Moses received the tables of the Law, but Simeon receives the Son in whose Incarnation the 'shadow' is replaced by the full reality of God's presence with his people. Mary and Joseph stand with their hands raised in a gesture of offering; this gesture includes the element of sacrifice that had to be offered for the ritual purification required by the Law, but the gesture is primarily one of offering the Incarnate Son to the representatives of the old covenant community of Israel; likewise we are reminded that the Mother of God offers her Son to all who will receive him with faith and love — those very qualities expressed in the outstretched arms of Simeon as he receives the Christ child.

The liturgical texts for the feast celebrate this meeting, and contain allusions to many themes and images in the Old Testament:

'Today the holy Mother who is higher than any temple, has come into the temple, disclosing to the world the Maker of the world and Giver of the Law. Simeon the Elder receives him in his arms and, venerating Him, he cries aloud: "Now lettest thou thy servant depart, for I have seen thee, the Saviour of our souls".'[20]

'Christ the coal of fire, whom Isaiah foresaw, now rests in the arms of the Theotokos as in a pair of tongs, and he is given to the Elder.' (see Isaiah 6.6)[21]

'Hail, O Theotokos Virgin full of grace: for from thee has shone forth the Sun of Righteousness, Christ our God, giving light to those in darkness. Be glad also, thou righteous Elder, for thou hast received in

Continued on page 143

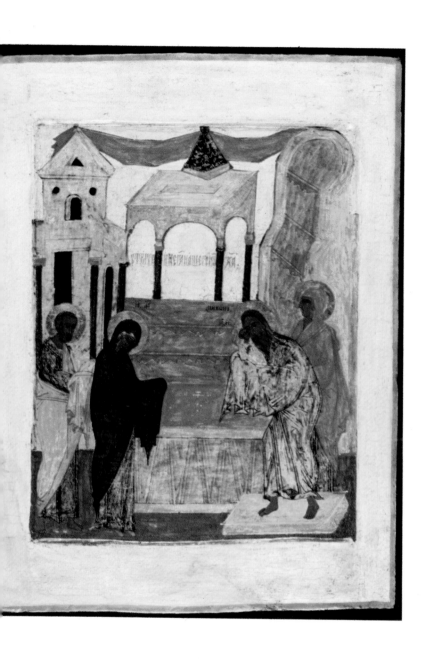

PLATE 12 *(opposite)*

THE ANNUNCIATION (Feast day, 25 March)

Moscow School; c.1500.
School of Dionysius.

St Luke's account of the Annunciation (Luke 1.26–38) has been the source of inspiration for a great deal of Christian art in both Eastern and Western Churches from the late second century onwards, and the theme of the Annunciation has a prominent place in popular devotion throughout Christendom. The Feast of the Annunciation celebrates the willingness of Mary to co-operate with the divine plan for the salvation of mankind; it is a feast that is full of the spirit of awe and joy — awe at the great mystery of the divine humility in taking our humanity, and joy at Mary's response of love and obedience which forms a major step in the accomplishment of our salvation. The colours used in this icon convey something of the wonder and joy that are associated with this feast.

The details of the iconography of this feast are drawn primarily from the Gospel of St Luke, but also from the Protevangelium of James (probably late second century). The Protevangelium elaborates on the infancy narratives of Matthew and Luke, and includes the story of Mary's parents Joachim and Anna, the conception and birth of the Virgin, her presentation and life in the Temple, and her betrothal to Joseph; we are also told that at the time of the Annunciation Mary was engaged in drawing out purple thread that was to be used for making a veil for the Temple. This latter detail is almost always included in icons of the Annunciation, often with the thread falling away to the ground: Mary turns away from the external work with the thread for a veil in the Jerusalem Temple, to attend to the vocation to become the temple and dwelling place of the Incarnate Lord.

In this icon the posture and gesture of Gabriel, the architectural features of the background, and the contrasting series of levels in the lower half of the icon all serve to focus attention on the one who is called to be the Theotokos — the God-bearer; but at the same time there is a tension between the two figures in the icon which keeps our attention on the nature of the event being set before us — the meeting between the messenger of God's plan for salvation and the one who has been chosen to be the means whereby the Incarnation may take place. Mary's posture represents interior concentration, and a questioning of both the angel and the message he brings — 'How can this be?' The Fathers of the Church often speak of Mary's

Continued on page 144

PLATE 13 *(opposite)*

THE RAISING OF LAZARUS (Feast day, Saturday before Palm Sunday)

Novgorod School; fifteenth century.

The account of the raising of Lazarus in chapter 11 of St John's Gospel is central to the whole of that Gospel. It is the last of the 'signs' of Jesus by which his glory is manifested before the final and greatest 'sign' — his death and resurrection *(see page 41)*. Before his own death and resurrection, Christ the Life-Giver raises Lazarus from the dead, and thereby precipitates the attack (John 11.49–53) that will lead to his death and resurrection, that final and conclusive 'sign' by which his glory is revealed. In the Gospel narrative the account of the event is permeated by profound symbolism and allusions to ideas and events mentioned elsewhere in St John's Gospel; in this icon some of the symbolism is given visual expression, and the icon brings into focus in one single composition the many details and levels of interpretation that are there in the Gospel narrative.

The bound figure of Lazarus stands out prominently against the dark background of the cave — that frequently recurring symbol of ignorance and unenlightened humanity, but also here emphasising the death which Lazarus has experienced. Christ is accompanied by some of the Jews and his own apostles, and approaches the cave. At his feet kneel Martha and Mary, the dead man's sisters, imploring the Lord's help; and above the two women two men take away the stone from the grave in obedience to the Lord's command.

There is no hint of the common segment of the celestial sphere as the source of the events portrayed in the icon; instead the figure of Christ — God Incarnate — together with the figure of Lazarus form the two major focal points within the icon. The distorted mountains are reminders that the event represented is one of major spiritual significance *(see pp.34 and 83)*. Below the blue 'uncreated light' of the highest level in the icon the whole scene is illuminated from the figure of Lazarus who is raised from the darkness of death to the enlightenment and illumination of the New Life bestowed by the Incarnate Life-Giver.

The Feast of the Raising of Lazarus is celebrated on the eve of Palm Sunday, thus preserving the close link between this event and the saving events of the Lord's Passion and Resurrection which are to be celebrated during Holy Week and Easter.

Four texts in St John's account of the raising of Lazarus point
Continued on page 145

PLATE 14 *(opposite)*
THE CRUCIFIXION
Northern Russian School; c.1600.

In the Orthodox tradition, the Crucifixion is celebrated primarily as the victory of the One who became incarnate for our salvation. The Victorious Cross is celebrated in poetry, liturgy and iconography because Christ's self oblation on the Cross was the means whereby the gates of Paradise can be opened for the sons and daughters of Adam. By his death he has destroyed death and overcome the power of evil; the darkness of the hour of Crucifixion is in fact the hour of triumph; Judas going out into the night to betray Christ was unwittingly preparing the way for the great work of atonement as the Incarnate Son who 'emptied himself' to share our life now enters into death to break the power of sin and death.

The early representations of the Cross of Christ are symbols of victory and triumph. In Baptism we enter into that life where we are called to take up our Cross and follow Christ in his passion and resurrection. The sacraments of Baptism and the Eucharist both proclaim the Lord's death as the way to life.

All this is utterly in keeping with St Paul's assertion in 1 Corinthians 17–25 that in the Cross of Christ we come face to face with the power and wisdom of God in a form that those outside the faith can only see as weakness and folly. The Cross is celebrated as life-giving, and from quite an early stage in Christian teaching becomes equated with the Tree of Life: the wood of the Cross where the Lord is put to death becomes the Tree of Life where Christians can receive the fruits of Christ's Passion and enter into the fulness of the heavenly life.

In this icon Christ is raised up on the Cross, to draw all men to Himself (John 12.32). The Crucifixion takes place outside the city walls of Jerusalem, in the place where, according to tradition, Adam has been buried. Thus the second Adam, Christ, willingly submits to death over the place where the first Adam was buried; the blood of the second Adam avails for the salvation of the whole world, including the salvation of the first Adam, and in many icons of the Crucifixion the skull of Adam is depicted in the cave beneath the Cross. Strange though some of these traditions may appear to Western Christians they express in visual and in story form the faith of the Bible and the Church that 'As in Adam all die, so also in Christ shall all be made alive' (1 Cor. 15.22).

On the right of the icon St John is grief stricken at the death of his
Continued on page 145

PLATE 15 *(opposite)*
THE ANASTASIS (The Harrowing of Hell)
Novgorod School; c.1500.

The theme of this icon is Christ's entering into the depths of the underworld; this is the full extent of his abasement and humiliation and at the same time the means of salvation to those who died before Christ (see Acts 2.22–33 and 1 Pet. 3.19). The Apocryphal Gospel of Nicodemus (second century) elaborates the imagery and details of this element of the faith on which the New Testament is rather more reticent:

> 'The gates of brass were broken in pieces and the bars of iron were crushed and all the dead who were buried were loosened from their chains . . . and the king of glory entered in like a man, and all the dark places of Hades were illuminated . . . The Saviour blessed Adam . . . and he did this also to the patriarchs, martyrs and forefathers and he took them and leapt out of Hades.'[35]

The liturgical texts for Holy Saturday make use of this imagery in the Church's worship:

> 'Today doth Hades groaning cry, My might is sacrificed. The Shepherd is crucified and Adam raised. Them that I ruled I have lost. Them I devoured in my power I have disgorged them all. The Crucified hath opened the graves, and the power of death hath no avail. Glory to thy Cross O Lord, and to thy Resurrection.'[36]

In this icon Christ is shown against the background of the mandorla descending to the realms of the dead, bearing in his left hand the life giving Cross, the symbol of the victory achieved by his death. Beneath his feet the gates of Hades are broken down. (Some icons of this theme show all the instruments of imprisonment — locks, keys, etc. — scattered beneath the broken doors). Christ grasps the wrist of Adam and raises him from the tomb; this subtle detail of the way Christ holds Adam indicates that it is Christ's work of redemption that raises Adam and the whole of fallen humanity into the new life of the Resurrection. On the right is Eve, and behind her and Adam are the kings and prophets of the Old Testament whose vocation was to prepare the way for the coming of the Saviour.

Icons of this theme can powerfully convey the full extent of Christ's redeeming power and love. (See Rom. 8.38–39 and Col. 1.13–20. *See also plate 18(ii) and pp.41–42).*

PLATE 16 *(opposite)*
THE TRANSFIGURATION OF CHRIST
(Feast day, 6 August)
Cretan School; sixteenth century.

The Feast of the Transfiguration celebrates the manifestation of Christ's glory to Peter, James and John. The event of the Transfiguration as told in the synoptic Gospels (Matt. 17.1–8; Mark 9.2–8; Luke 9.28–36) comes shortly after the first prediction of the Passion, and provides for these three apostles a glimpse of the glory of the incarnate Son before the Passion that has been foretold and willingly accepted by Christ, and before the final glory of the Resurrection. The disciples see Christ transfigured; they see Moses and Elijah with Christ; the cloud overshadows them; and they hear the voice from the cloud, 'This is my beloved Son, listen to him'.

The liturgical texts of the Feast celebrate the revelation of the divine nature of Christ in this mysterious event. He is the one who fulfils the law and the prophets, and leads his people to behold his glory.

'Going up with the disciples into the mountain, Thou hast shone forth with the glory of the Father. Moses and Elijah stood at Thy side, for the Law and the prophets minister to Thee as God. And the Father, acknowledging Thy natural Sonship, called Thee Son. We praise Him in song together with Thee and the spirit.'[37]

'Enlightening the disciples that were with Thee, O Christ our Benefactor, Thou hast shown them upon the holy mountain the hidden and blinding light of Thy nature and of Thy divine beauty beneath the flesh; and they, understanding that Thy glory could not be borne, loudly cried out, "Holy art Thou". For Thou art He whom no man may approach, yet wast Thou seen in the flesh by the world, O Thou who alone lovest mankind.'[38]

'Having uncovered, O Saviour, a little of the light of Thy divinity to those who went up with Thee into the mountain, Thou hast made them lovers of Thy heavenly glory. Therefore they cried in awe: "It is good for us to be here." With them we also sing unto Thee, O Saviour Christ who wast transfigured.'[39]

'Thou wast transfigured upon the mountain, and Thy disciples beheld Thy glory, O Christ our God, as far as they were able to do so: that when they saw Thee crucified, they might know that Thy suffering was voluntary, and might proclaim unto the world that Thou art truly the Brightness of the Father.'[40]

In this icon Christ stands on the central mountain peak; the mandorla behind him indicates the divine nature which is manifest

Continued on page 146

PLATE 17 *(opposite)*

THE DORMITION OF THE MOTHER OF GOD
(Feast day, 15 August)

Moscow School; early sixteenth century.

In Eastern and Western Churches the fifteenth of August is kept as the feast that celebrates the entry of the Blessed Virgin Mary into heaven; it marks the end of her earthly life and is a celebration of the vocation of all Christian people to share fully in Christ in the joys of heaven. The feast of the Dormition in the Orthodox Churches concentrates on the death of the Theotokos and the traditions associated with that event: the assembly of the apostles from far and wide, and the sense of awe and wonder as she who has been the God-bearer commends her soul to the God she had borne in her womb. According to the tradition honoured in the Eastern Churches St Thomas did not arrive until after the death and burial of Mary, and it was his visit to her tomb near the Garden of Gethsemane that led to the revelation of the Assumption of her body into heaven. Here again we have traditions that may seem strange to some Western Christians, but the dogmatic point is clearly stated: she who bore the Incarnate Son has been given a full share in the Resurrection life, and received body and soul into heaven to share in the glory that awaits all those who look forward to the perfection of Christ's work of redemption.

The liturgical texts of the Feast of the Dormition express the details of the event and its spiritual significance as seen through the eyes of the Orthodox Churches:

> 'At thy departing, O Virgin Theotokos, to him who was ineffably born of thee, James the first bishop and brother of the Lord was there, and so was Peter, the honoured leader and chief of the disciples, and the whole sacred fellowship of the apostles . . . They sang the praises of the divine and amazing mystery of the dispensation of Christ our God; and the rejoiced, O far-famed Virgin, as they buried thy body, the origin of the Life and holder of God. On high the most holy and venerable of the angelic powers bowed in wonder before this marvel, and said to one another: "Open wide your gates and receive her who bore the Creator of heaven and earth".[41]
>
> 'Sing, O ye people, sing ye the praises of the Mother of our God: for today she delivers her soul, full of light, into the immaculate hands of him who was made incarnate of her without seed. And she entreats him without ceasing to grant the inhabited earth peace and great mercy.'[42]
>
> 'Having become the Temple of Life, thou hast obtained the life

Continued on page 147

THE KARIYE CAMII, ISTANBUL

The Kariye Camii is the Turkish name for the famous Church of the Saviour in Chora. It was a monastery church outside the old city walls of Constantinople, looking out into the countryside. (The Greek 'chora' means land or countryside). The site has had a long history as a church but became a mosque in 1511 ('Camii' is Turkish for mosque); it is now a museum. The Kariye Camii is particularly important for its remarkable mosaics and frescoes that were executed in the church in the early fourteenth century (c.1315–21) at a time when the Paleologue revival of artistic work was at its height. The work was under the patronage of a very wealthy and learned government official, Theodore Metochites. The art of this church is remarkable for its vitality and attention to details of great human interest. There is a great warmth and humanity in this work, without a departure from the spiritual and dogmatic intentions of Orthodox iconography.

(i) This figure of Christ is a mosaic panel; fortunately the main figure is intact, though the edges of the panel have lost many of the tesserae used to make up the mosaic composition. The use of very small tesserae of different materials and colours enabled the artists responsible for the Kariye Camii mosaics to achieve very subtle gradations of colour and texture. The main lines of this composition are bold and definite, forming a structure within which there is much subtlety of colour. Christ's gaze does not have the severity often expressed in similar compositions; placed above the door between the two narthexes of the church, this figure of Christ welcomes those who enter the building. The right hand is held in the familiar gesture of blessing and is turned towards the heart, while the left hand holds the jewel-studded book. The silhouette of the figure is completely unbroken, and helps to convey the striking sense of inner concentration and energy. Beneath the initials for Jesus Christ is the inscription 'The Land of the Living', which is repeated on a similar mosaic panel of Christ above the entrance to the Church itself. All around the narthexes are scenes from the life of the Virgin and the life of Christ. Two particular scenes are placed above this figure of Christ at the entrance to the second narthex: the wedding at Cana with the filling of the waterpots, and the multiplication of the loaves with the distribution of the bread to the hungry crowd. These two scenes indicate many different aspects of the truth of Christ: his fulfilment of the Old Covenant with the New; the marriage feast as a

Continued on page 148

141

Continued from page 112
assembled around an unseen circle — the shape of the mandorla often used to represent the divine source of the particular revelation given in icons of the Transfiguration of Christ, the Harrowing of Hell, and the Dormition of the Virgin. Unity and diversity are held together in Rublev's composition, representing the perfection of communion and mutual love within the Holy Trinity, and the mutual involvement of each Person of the Trinity in the work of revelation and redemption.

The icon reproduced here belongs to the tradition that was shaped by Rublev's great work, but has more details included on the table, and a more prominent portrayal of the home, the tree and the mountain. Even though the circle is less dominant as a hidden structural element in this icon, there is a strong sense of harmony, communion, and participation in the life of the Holy Trinity.

Continued from page 122
The Virgin Mother lies in the centre of the icon, as the second Eve. Just as the first Eve was the 'mother of all living' (Gen 3.20), so the Virgin Mother of God is the Mother of the new humanity restored and deified through the Incarnation of the Eternal Son.

The angels praise and glorify God, and also bring the message to the shepherds, one of whom looks up in wonder while the other plays his pipe in celebration. If the shepherds symbolize simple folk and the Jewish people, the Magi symbolize wise and learned people, and the Gentile nations; they are shown as of different ages, making the point that the reception of the salvation and revelation given in Christ is not dependent on such external factors as maturity of years.

Below the Virgin, midwives deal with the practical consequences of a human birth — the washing of the baby. According to the apocryphal Gospels of pseudo-Matthew and pseudo-James, Joseph hired midwives to help; their function in the icon is to stress the true humanity of the Incarnate God, against heretical teaching that Christ only appeared to be human.

At the bottom left corner of the icon sits Joseph, the one who is not the father of the child, and who represents those who cannot comprehend the wonder of this event which is beyond the natural order of things. In some icons the devil disguised as an old shepherd stands in front of Joseph tempting him to disbelief. The face of the Virgin is turned towards Joseph — a symbol of compassion for those beset by doubts and difficulties in believing.

The homely details in this icon and its rich colouring help to convey something of the joy of this Feast.

'Thou hast shone forth from a Virgin, O Christ, Thou spiritual Sun of Righteousness. And a star showed Thee, whom nothing can contain, contained within a cave. Thou hast led the Magi to worship Thee, and joining them we magnify Thee: O Giver of Life, glory to Thee.'[13]

Continued from page 124

Imagery related to the Jordan, water, and the themes of Old and New Covenants:

'The river Jordan once turned back before the mantle of Elisha, after Elijah had been taken up into heaven, and the waters were divided on this side and on that (2 Kings 2.14); the stream became a dry path before him, forming a true figure of the baptism whereby we pass over the changeful course of life. Christ has appeared in the Jordan to sanctify the waters.'[16]

The manifestation of the Holy Trinity:

'The Trinity, our God, has today made itself indivisibly manifest to us. For the Father in a loud voice bore clear witness to his Son; the Spirit in the form of a dove came down from the sky; while the Son bent his immaculate head before the Forerunner, and by receiving baptism, he delivered us from bondage, in his love for mankind.'[17]

The gift of enlightenment, restoration and new life to the baptized:

'Come ye and let us go in spirit to the Jordan, there to see a great sight. For Jesus our Enlightenment approaches and bows his head beneath the hand of a servant . . . The living coal that Isaiah foresaw (Isa 6.6) is kindled in the waters of the Jordan, and he will burn up the whole substance of sin and grant restoration to the broken.'[18]

'O Word all-shining, sent forth from the Father,
Thou art come to dispel utterly the dark and evil night
And the sins of mortal men,
And by thy baptism to draw up with thee, O blessed Lord,
Bright sons from the streams of Jordan.'[19]

For the biblical texts relating to the Baptism of the Lord, see Matthew 3.13–17; Mark 1.9–11; Luke 3.21–22.

Continued from page 126

thine arms the Deliverer of our souls, who bestows upon us resurrection.'[22]

'"Thou hast committed to me the exceeding joy of thy salvation, O Christ", cried Simeon. "Take thy servant, who is weary of the shadow, and make him a new preacher of the mystery of grace, as he magnifies thee in praise."'[23]

143

The architectural setting of the incident in this icon indicates the Temple with the altar and the canopy, but it can also indicate the interior world of the human soul and consciousness where we too are to meet the Incarnate Son and welcome with joy him who comes to dwell with his people.

> 'O Christ our God, who hast been pleased to rest this day in the arms of the Elder as upon the chariot of the cherubim, from the tyranny of the passions now deliver us who sing thy praises, and save our souls.'[24]

Continued from page 128
obedience as marking the reversal of the consequences of Eve's disobedience (Gen. 3); and part of the liturgical texts for this feast portray Mary's unwillingness to be beguiled by the angelic messenger: 'I am filled with joy at thy word, yet am afraid: I fear lest thou deceive me, as Eve was deceived, and lead me far from God'. God's choice of Mary is balanced by Mary's conscious choice of co-operation; the 'second Eve' makes the answer that brings the 'new Adam' into the world, and leads to our salvation and participation in the life of the Holy Trinity.

The texts of this feast celebrate both the event and its significance for the salvation of mankind:

> 'Today is revealed the mystery that is from all eternity. The Son of God becomes the Son of man, that, sharing in what is worse, He may make me share in what is better. In times of old Adam was once deceived: he sought to become God, but received not his desire. Now God becomes man, that he may make Adam God. Let creation rejoice, let nature exult: for the Archangel stands in fear before the Virgin and, saying to her "Hail", he brings the joyful greeting whereby our sorrow is assuaged. O Thou who in thy merciful compassion wast made man, our God, glory to Thee.'[25]

> 'O marvel! God is come among men; he who cannot be contained is contained in a womb; the Timeless enters time; and. strange wonder! his conception is without seed, his emptying past telling: so great is this mystery! For God empties himself, takes flesh, and is fashioned as a creature, when the angel tells the pure Virgin of her conception: "Hail, thou who art full of grace: the Lord who has great mercy is with thee".'[26]

> 'Hail, O Theotokos, deliverance from the curse of Adam. Hail, holy Mother of God; hail, living Bush. Hail, Lamp; hail, Throne; hail Ladder and Gate. Hail, divine Chariot; hail, swift Cloud. Hail, Temple; hail, Vessel of Gold. Hail, Mountain; hail, Tabernacle and Table. Hail, thou release of Eve.'[27]

(See Gen. 3.15–17; Exod 3.2; 25.31; Gen. 28.12, 17; Ezek 44.2; Isa 19.1; Exod 16.33; Dan 2.34–35; Exod 26.1; 25.23)

This icon sets before us the mystery of the Annunciation in order that its significance may be mediated to the souls of those who pray before the icon. As we honour Mary's openness to God and co-operation with his plan for our salvation, we pray that our own vocation may be honoured with the same courage, humility and love.

Continued from page 130
beyond the external, public event which the Feast celebrates, to insights about our redemption and participation in the Life of Christ.

> 'I am the resurrection and the life; he who believes in me, though he die, yet shall he live; and whoever lives and believes in me shall never die.' (11.26)

St John shows Christ before his Passion and Resurrection speaking of himself as the Resurrection and the Life. The Sacraments and our private devotion are the means whereby we participate in that life, and are raised up into Christ. See quotations from Nicholas Cabasilas *The Life of Christ* given earlier (*pp.59–61*).

'Lazarus, come forth' (11.43). The summons of Christ to Lazarus is the same to each one of us: to come forth from a life overshadowed by the darkness of death, sin and ignorance, into the freedom and light of Christ's presence and revelation.

'Take the stone away' (11.39) and 'Unbind him and let him go' (11.44). Christ uses the work of other people to free Lazarus into life, and our experience of salvation in Christ includes the ministry of others in removing the elements that block our way into the life that is transfigured by God's grace; for example, in receiving teaching, and in receiving sacramental absolution.

> 'Before Thine own death, O Christ, Thou has raised from hell Lazarus that was four days dead, and hast shaken the dominion of death. Through this one man whom Thou hast loved, Thou hast foretold the deliverance of all men from corruption. We therefore worship Thine almighty power and cry: Blessed art Thou, O Saviour, have mercy upon us.'[28]

Continued from page 132
Lord; behind him stands the centurion who confessed Christ as the Son of God. On the left of the icon stands the Mother of God, with

145

her right hand in a gesture of pointing towards her crucified Son, and indicating the saving mystery of his death. Behind Mary stands one of the holy women whose right hand also directs our attention to the Saviour of the world.

With its quiet harmony of colour and balanced composition this icon points us to the spiritual tradition that sees 'blessed dispassion' as part of the goal of the life of prayer, Christ on the Cross is the exemplar of the life that is freed from the passions. 'A man is truly dispassionate . . . when he has lifted his mind above everything created, and has made it master of all the senses; where he keeps his soul continually in the presence of the Lord.' (St John Climacus)

The following quotations from the liturgical texts for the feast of the Exaltation of the Cross and Good Friday will illustrate the attitude to the Cross that lies at the heart of Orthodox devotion to the Cross of Christ.

> 'Today he who is by nature unapproachable, becomes approachable for me, and suffers his Passion, thus setting me free from passions.'[29]
> 'Lifted high upon the Cross, O Master, with thyself thou hast raised up Adam and the whole of fallen nature.'[30]
> 'The Tree of true life was planted in the place of the skull, and upon it hast thou, the eternal king, worked salvation in the midst of the earth.'[31]
> 'Hail! life-giving Cross, unconquerable trophy of Godliness, door to Paradise, succour of the faithful, rampart set about the Church. Through thee corruption is utterly destroyed, the power of death is swallowed up, and we are raised from earth to heaven.'[32]
> 'Hail! Guide of the blind, physician of the sick and resurrection of all the dead. O precious Cross, thou hast lifted us up when we were fallen into mortality.'[33]
> 'For my sake Thou wast crucified, to become for me a fountain of forgiveness. Thy side was pierced, that Thou mightest pour upon me streams of life. Thou wast transfixed with nails, that through the depth of Thy sufferings I might know with certainty the height of Thy power, and cry to Thee, O Christ Giver of Life: O Saviour, glory to Thy Cross and Passion.'[34]

Continued from page 136
in him. On either side of Christ are Moses (right) and Elijah (left) representing the law and the prophets, and pointing to Christ whose coming death and resurrection will inaugurate the New Covenant foreshadowed in and prepared for by the law and the prophets. In the lower part of the icon Peter, John and James are shown overwhelmed by the glory they have beheld; Peter shields his eyes with his left hand, and with his right hand points to Christ; John and

James fall away from the sight of the transfigured Christ, and their sandals fall from their feet. The icon has a strong sense of balance and harmony, both in design and in the use of colours. The focal point of attention is the transfigured Christ in whom 'all the fulness of God was pleased to dwell' (Col. 1.19), the beloved Son to whom we must listen.

The Feast of the Transfiguration is one of major significance in Orthodox theology and spirituality. It is a celebration of the glory of Christ, the glory of the one who brings to the world the light of divine revelation and entrusts it to his Church as the means whereby we can enter into the glory of Christ's transfigured humanity.

> 'And we all, with unveiled face, beholding the glory of the Lord, are being changed into his likeness, from one degree of glory to another.' (2 Cor. 3.18)

Continued from page 138

> eternal: for thou who hast borne the Life in Person, hast now passed over through death into life.'[43]
>
> 'Neither the tomb nor death had power over the Theotokos, who is ever watchful in her prayers and in whose intercession lies unfailing hope. For as the Mother of Life she has been transported into life by him who dwelt within her ever-virgin womb.'[44]

This icon, with its quiet and tranquil harmony of form and colour shows the apostles gathered around the dead body of the Virgin; St Peter is on the left holding a censer and St Paul bows low over the feet of the Virgin; the four bishops shown with haloes are St James, the first Bishop of Jerusalem, Timothy, Heirotheus and Dionysius the Areopagite; behind the bishops various holy women complete the assembly. Above the body of the Virgin stands the figure of Christ surrounded by a mandorla, and holding in his hands a figure in white representing the soul of the Virgin; heavenly powers surround the mandorla and gaze in adoration at the mystery of the Dormition.

In this icon, as in others reproduced in this book, we have a calm and powerful statement of the Christian hope of sharing in the glory of Christ. Yet the icon is not primarily addressed to our need to look for hope beyond the grave; that hope is given as we contemplate this particular aspect of the mystery of the Incarnation: she who held the Incarnate Word in her womb and in her arms now commends her soul to her creator and redeemer Lord, and is received into the glory of the heavenly realm.

Continued from page 140

symbol of the Messianic Banquet foreshadowed and anticipated in the Eucharist; the Bread of Life symbolized in the feeding miracles and received in the Eucharist. Thus this mosaic leads us to an understanding of Christ, the Christian and the Church: here in this church building one is entering into the land (chora) of the living, entering into the heavenly Kingdom of Christ, and in the Eucharist receiving the Bread of Life and the Wine of heaven.

(ii) On the south side of the main church is the Parecclesion or funerary chapel which is decorated with frescoes, in contrast to the mosaics of the main church and its two narthexes. In the apse of the parecclesion is this dramatic frescoe of the Anastasis; this traditional theme is here used to occupy the whole of the upper part of the apse, where the size and shape of the setting help to create the profound impact that is made by this fresco. It is remarkable for the delicacy of the facial details and the subtlety of the colours, (rarely, it seems, reproduced accurately); but the whole composition is permeated with a sense of spiritual power and urgency as the cosmic significance of Christ's death and resurrection are portrayed. Death and Hades cannot withstand the power of the Crucified Lord who conquers sin and death, and raises Adam and Eve into the glory of the resurrection life.

> 'Let no-one fear death, for our Saviour's death hath liberated us. He who was bound by it hath extinguished it. Descending into hades, he made hades captive . . . Christ hath arisen, and life reigneth.' (St John Chrysostom)[45]

(*see also plate 15, and pp.41-42*).

REFERENCES

Chapter 2 Historical Background: Beginnings and early developments

1. The *Painter's Manual* of Dionysius of Fourna, translated by Paul Hetherington (The Sagittarius Press, London, 1981) p.4.
2. Procopius, *Works*, translated by H.B. Dewing. Vol. vii (*Buildings*) (William Heinemann Ltd, London 1940) pp.13–27.
3. Quoted in Leonid Ouspensky *Theology of the Icon* (St Vladimir's Seminary Press, New York, 1978) p.103.
4. Ibid., p.104.

Chapter 3 Historical Background: The Triumph of Orthodoxy and later developments.

1. Quoted by Kallistos Ware in *Eastern Churches Review*, (Clarendon Press, Oxford) Vol viii, No.1, 1976, p.9.
2. St Theodore the Studite, *On the Holy Icons*, translated by Catharine P. Roth (St Vladimir's Seminary Press, New York, 1981) p.24.
3. Ibid., p.27.
4. Ibid., p.30.
5. Ibid., p.37.
6. Quoted in Ouspensky, op. cit., p.164 and p.166.
7. St Theodore op. cit., p. 21 and p.107.
8. Quoted in Ouspensky, op. cit., p.55.
9. Dionysius, op. cit., p.87.

Chapter 5 Biblical Interpretation: Allegory and the influence of Alexandrian Christianity

1. Philo of Alexandria, *The Contemplative Life, The Giants, and Selections*, in SPCK series, The Classics of Western Spirituality (London, 1981), p.81.

2. Ibid., p.81.
3. Ibid., p.46.
4. Ibid., p.55.
5. Origen, *On First Principles*, in *Origen, An Exhortation to Martyrdom, Prayer and Selected Works*, in SPCK series The Classics of Western Spirituality (London, 1979) p.182.
6. Ibid., p.187.
7. Ibid., p.192.
8. Ibid., p.202.
9. Ibid., p.180.
10. Ibid., p.181.
11. Ibid., p.180.
12. Quoted in *Alexandrian Christianity*, by John Oulton and Henry Chadwick, Vol. II of SCM Library of Christian Classics, (1954) p.18.
13. Ibid., p.21.

Chapter 6 The Spirituality of the Icon Painters

1. Quoted in Timothy Ware, *The Orthodox Church* (Pelican, 1963) p.224.
2. Gregory of Nyssa, *The Life of Moses*, The Classics of Western Spirituality series (Paulist Press, New York, 1978) p.83.
3. Ibid., p.85.
4. Nicholas Cabasilas, *The Life in Christ* (St Vladimir's Seminary Press, New York, 1974) pp.190–191.
5. Ibid., pp.43–44.
6. Ibid., pp.47–48.
7. Ibid., pp.48–49.
8. Ibid., pp.49–50.
9. Dionysius, op. cit., p.82.
10. St John Climacus, *The Ladder of Divine Ascent*, SPCK series The Classics of Western Spirituality (London, 1982) p.262.
11. Ibid., p.264.
12. Ibid., p.270.
13. Ibid., p.277.
14. Ibid., p.279.
15. Ibid., p.281.
16. Ibid., p.281.
17. Ibid., p.282.

18. Ibid., p.284.
19. Ibid., p.285.
20. Ibid., p.287.
21. Ibid., p.289.
22. *The Philokalia*, The Complete Text, Vol. I. Translated from the Greek and edited by G.E.H. Palmer, Philip Sherrard, and Kallistos Ware (Faber and Faber, London and Boston, 1979) p.182.
23. Ibid., p.185.
24. Ibid., p.57.
25. Ibid., p.63.
26. Ibid., p.64.
27. Ibid., p.175.
28. Ibid., p.195.
29. Ibid., p.61.
30. Ibid., p.66.
31. Ibid., p.166.
32. Ibid., p.167.
33. Ibid., p.183.
34. Ibid., p.293.
35. Ibid., p.244.
36. Ibid., p.270.
37. Ibid., p.253.
38. Ibid., p.65.
39. Ibid., p.66.
40. Ibid., p.176.
41. Ibid., p.176.
42. Ibid., p.276.
43. Ibid., p.166.
44. Ibid., p.255.
45. Ibid., p.26.
46. Ibid., p.63.
47. Ibid., p.175.
48. Ibid., p.162.
49. Ibid., p.163.
50. Ibid., p.163.
51. Ibid., p.164.
52. Ibid., p.166.
53. Ibid., p.178.
54. Ibid., p.196.
55. Ibid., p.197.
56. Ibid., p.293.

Chapter 7 The Visual Language of Icons

1. Dionysius, op. cit., p.32.
2. Ibid., p.33.
3. Ibid., p.87.
4. Ibid., p.50.
5. Ibid., p.32.
6. Ibid., p.53.
7. Ibid., p.87.

Chapter 8 Icons and their environment

1. Quoted in T. Ware, op. cit., p.269.
2. *The Orthodox Liturgy*, (SPCK 1964) p.89.
3. Quoted in T. Ware, op. cit., p.77.
4. Maxim Gorky, *My Childhood* (Pelican Classics, 1966), pp.61, 62 and 64.

Commentary on the Plates

1. *The Philokalia*, op. cit., p.195.
2. St John Climacus, op. cit., p.264.
3. *The Philokalia*, op. cit., p.270.
4. Ibid., p.26.
5. Ibid., p.164.
6. St John Climacus, op. cit., p.264.
7. *The Philokalia*, op. cit., p.185.
8. Ibid., p.163.
9. Ibid., p.255.
10. *The Festal Menaion*, translated from the original Greek by Mother Mary and Archimandrite Kallistos Ware (Faber and Faber, London, 1977) p.277.
11. Ibid., p.214.
12. Ibid., p.254.
13. Ibid., p.260.
14. Ibid., p.383.
15. Ibid., p.296.
16. Ibid., p.296–297.
17. Ibid., p.322.

18. Ibid., p.309.
19. Ibid., p.371.
20. Ibid., p.407.
21. Ibid., p.407.
22. Ibid., pp.416–417.
23. Ibid., p.426.
24. Ibid., p.429.
25. Ibid., p.460.
26. Ibid., p.443–444.
27. Ibid., p.459.
28. *The Lenten Triodion*, translated from the original Greek by Mother Mary and Archimandrite Kallistos Ware (Faber & Faber, London 1978) p.486.
29. *The Festal Menaion*, op. cit., p.158.
30. Ibid., p.131.
31. Ibid., p.137.
32. Ibid., pp.139–140.
33. Ibid., p.140.
34. *The Lenten Triodion*, op. cit., pp.589–590.
35. Henneke, *New Testament Apocrypha*, (Lutterworth Press, 1963).
36. *Euchology: Prayers of the Orthodox Church*, translated by G.V. Shann (Kidderminster 1891), p.363.
37. *The Festal Menaion*, op. cit., p.479.
38. Ibid., pp.479–480.
39. Ibid., p.481.
40. Ibid., p.489.
41. Ibid., p.511.
42. Ibid., p.510.
43. Ibid., p.520.
44. Ibid., p.520.
45. St John Chrysostom, Catechical Discourse in *Euchology*, op. cit., p.392.

FURTHER READING

ICONS AND CHRISTIAN ART
M V Alpatov: *Early Russian Icon Painting*, Moscow 1978
H P Gerhard: *The World of Icons*. John Murray 1971
Andre Grabar: *Christian Iconography: a Study of its origins*. Routledge and Kegan Paul 1969 and 1980
Andre Grabar: *Byzantine Painting*. Macmillan, London 1979
Jean Lassus: *The Early Christian and Byzantine World*. Paul Hamlyn, London 1967
Leonid Ouspensky: *Theology of the Icon*. St Vladimir's Seminary Press 1978
Leonid Ouspensky and Vladimir Lossky: *The Meaning of Icons*. St Vladimir's Seminary Press 1982
Steven Runciman: *Byzantine Style and Civilization*. Penguin Books Ltd. 1975
John Stuart: *Icons*. Faber and Faber 1975
David Talbot Rice: *Art of the Byzantine Era*. Thames and Hudson, London 1963
Kurt Weitzmann: *The Icon*. Chatto and Windus 1978
Kurt Weitzmann and others: *The Icon*. Evans Brothers Ltd. 1982
Munemoto Yanagi and others: *Byzantium*. Cassell, London 1978

ORTHODOX CHURCH, THEOLOGY, SPIRITUALITY, ETC.
Pierre Kovalevsky: *Saint Sergius and Russian Spirituality*. St Vladimir's Seminary Press 1976
Vladimir Lossky: *The Vision of God*. The Faith Press 1963
Vladimir Lossky: *The Mystical Theology of the Eastern Church*. James Clark and Co Ltd., London 1957
Vladimir Lossky: *In the Image and Likeness of God*. A R Mowbray and Co Ltd., London and Oxford 1975
A Monk of the Eastern Church: *Orthodox Spirituality*. SPCK, London 1980
G E H Palmer, Philip Sherrard and Kallistos Ware: *Translation of complete text of the Philokalia in three volumes*. Faber and Faber 1979
Philip Sherrard: *Athos, The Holy Mountain*. Sidgwick and Jackson, London 1982
Kallistos Ware: *The Orthodox Church*, Pelican Books 1963
Kallistos Ware: *The Orthodox Way*, A R Mowbray and Co Ltd. 1979

Works quoted in the book are also recommended for further reading.

INDEX